HIT IT!

Your complete guide to Water Skiing

Bruce Kistler, MS

Former Director
American Water Ski Association

Leisure Press
Champaign, Illinois

Developmental Editor: June I. Decker, PhD
Copy Editor: Wendy Nelson
Assistant Editor: JoAnne Cline
Production Director: Ernie Noa
Projects Manager: Lezli Harris
Typesetter: Brad Colson
Text Design: Keith Blomberg
Text Layout: Tara Welsch and Michelle Baum
Cover Design: Jack Davis
Cover Photo: Tom King
Illustrations By: Carol Ritter
Printed By: Versa Press

ISBN: 0-88011-313-8

Copyright © 1988 by Bruce Kistler

Library of Congress Cataloging-in-Publication Data

Kistler, Bruce, 1951-
    Hit it! : your complete guide to water skiing / Bruce Kistler.
        p.   cm.
    ISBN 0-88011-313-8
    1. Water skiing.   I. Title.
GV840.S5K57 1988
797.3'5–dc19   88-8601
                                                                CIP

Printed in the United States of America

10 9 8 7 6 5 4 3 2 1

Leisure Press
A Division of Human Kinetics Publishers, Inc.
Box 5076, Champaign, IL 61820
1-800-342-5457
1-800-334-3665 (in Illinois)

To Susan with love.

TABLE
OF CONTENTS

FOREWORD

It's hard to beat water skiing as a recreational activity. It's fun for the whole family, it's good exercise, and it's a great way to enjoy America's waterways. I know this from personal experience.

Water skiing is also a great competitive sport that teaches the value of goal setting, hard work, and sportsmanship. This, too, I know from personal experience.

When I was in high school and college, I competed in track and field hoping that someday I would be good enough to get to the Olympics. During the summers, though, the sport I chose to compete in was water skiing. I had a lot of fun at the tournaments and I enjoyed many good times with my fellow competitors, including Bruce Kistler, the author of this book.

Bruce has written a book that can be of untold value to the beginning and intermediate water skier. If you have never been on water skis before, *Hit It!* can help take the frustration out of getting up the first time. If you already know how to ski, it can teach you skills that will help you get the full enjoyment out of different types of water skiing like slalom, tricks, and barefooting. If you dream of skiing in tournaments, Bruce has explained the basic rules and given you some advice on how to get started in competition. *Hit It!* also contains valuable information for water ski towboat drivers and those who want to teach others how to ski. There is a strong emphasis on safety throughout the text.

You'll have to practice hard to get proficient at water skiing, but with *Hit It!* you'll learn even quicker than I did. Best wishes and good luck!

Bruce Jenner

ACKNOWLEDGMENTS

I would like to thank the following people for their assistance during the preparation of this book:

For providing the equipment used in the photographs and for helping to defray the cost of the photography and the line drawings, I thank Bill Wiesner, president and general manager of O'Brien International; Chuck West, president of Mastercraft Boats; and Tom Casad, president of Casad Manufacturing Corporation.

For graciously allowing the use of their fine ski school facilities as a photography location, I thank Chuck and Sharon Dees of Dees Ski Centre of Auburndale, Florida. (Chuck also served as the towboat driver model.) Thanks also to Dees Ski Centre employees Brian Lamb, Sandy Martin, and Jackie Nanette for all their help and cooperation.

Thank you to Jenny Bosold, Travis Dees, Stephanie Maddox, and Mike Miller, for their patience and hard work as the principal skier models; Steve Holton, for driving the towboat for most of the photographs; photographer Tom King and graphic artist Carol Ritter, for lending their professional polish to the illustrations; and veteran boating writer Tom Hardman, for his advice during the preparation of the book proposal.

Lastly, I would like to thank "Big Al" McGrath, without whose help many years ago I would not have been able to pursue such an active interest in water skiing, and my parents for supporting and encouraging me in that pursuit.

CHAPTER 1

WELCOME TO THE WORLD OF WATER SKIING

Each summer, from the rivers of Wisconsin to the lakes of central Florida and from the reservoirs of North Carolina to the bays of California, millions of Americans enjoy water skiing. Although no one knows for sure, there are probably more water-skiers in the United States (about 18 million) than in all other countries of the world combined. This is partly because America is blessed with both an abundance of waterways that are open to public recreation and a high standard of living that puts a powerboat and a pair of skis within the financial reach of many families.

But what is it about water skiing that people find so attractive? What makes it so much fun? One answer is that water skiing allows you to freely and safely experience the exhilaration of speed. Rarely is the thrill of going fast as pure and free. You must rely on a boat for propulsion, of course, but the boat is your servant. The towrope is not a tether but a source of power for you to use. What is more, you can enjoy the sensation of speed without risking life and limb. Because water is forgiving, falls become part of the fun. The jostling you receive in a spill is just a reminder that your mastery of speed is never perfect.

Feeling free and going fast only partly account for the magic of water skiing. The physical setting of the waterbody and its mood—which can be changed in an instant by wind and weather—are an integral part

1

Figure 1.1. Water skiing means wholesome family fun.

of the experience. Whether slicing across a mirror-smooth mountain lake at sunrise or skipping like a stone over a wave-tossed coastal bay at noon, on water skis you sense the beauty of your aquatic surroundings directly and intimately.

Water skiing is an individual sport that appeals to the independent-minded, yet it is very much a social activity that is ideal for families and groups of friends (Figure 1.1). Water skiing is good exercise that works muscles rarely used in daily life. A very relaxing form of recreation or a demanding test of athletic skill, depending on how vigorously it is pursued, water skiing is a lifetime sport that can be enjoyed from the time one is a toddler until old age.

The Origins and Growth of Water Skiing

Following the end of World War I, the sport of aquaplaning emerged as a pastime, particularly in resort areas where boating was popular. The forerunner of the water ski, an aquaplane is a wide board that is towed directly by the boat like a sled. A large planing area was necessary then, because the displacement-type motorboats of that era were not very fast.

Figure 1.2.   Ralph Samuelson, the Father of Water Skiing.

The first person to ride on a pair of water skis as we know them was Ralph Samuelson in 1922 at Lake City, Minnesota. Believing that if people could ski on snow, they could also ski on water, Samuelson first tried to ski on barrel staves, then on snow skis. Having no luck with these, he finally fashioned a pair of skis 8 feet long and 9 inches wide from pine boards and attached leather straps to them to hold his feet. For a towrope he used a long sash cord with a rubber-wrapped metal ring tied on the end for a handle (Figure 1.2).

As curious townsfolk gathered on shore, the adventurous 18-year-old tried day after day to get up behind a 24-foot motor launch. After much struggling and experimentation, he finally got up.

To the locals, who thought he would never succeed, Samuelson was a sensation. He went on to learn many stunts, like skiing on one ski and even jumping over a homemade jump ramp greased with lard. Samuelson's fame really spread when he started skiing behind an amphibious airplane that sometimes lifted him completely off the water! For a number of years the young daredevil put on one-man exhibitions in Michigan and Palm Beach, Florida, as well as throughout Minnesota.

Unaware of Samuelson's exploits, others soon made the transition from aquaplaning to water skiing. On Long Island Sound in 1924, Fred Waller experimented with conventional skis like Samuelson's and with skis that were towed directly by the boat by means of a bridle, like an aquaplane split in half. In 1925 Waller patented his bridle-type "Akwa-Skees" because he believed that they were easier to ride than the others. On the other side of the country in Bellevue, Washington, Don Ibsen succeeded in riding his own homemade skis in 1928. At the same time in Miami Beach, Dick Pope (who later founded Cypress Gardens) and his brother Malcomb used bridle-type skis in exhibitions they staged for newsreel cameramen.

Water skiing may have been introduced to Europe by French vacationers who witnessed Samuelson's exhibitions in Florida, or it may have evolved there independently. In any case, water skiing was being enjoyed on the Continent as early as 1929.

Water skiing remained largely an exhibition stunt until 1939, when Dan B. Hains and a group of his friends organized the American Water Ski Association (AWSA) and produced the first National Water Ski Championships at Jones Beach State Park on Long Island. Although primitive by today's standards, the tournament included the three events of slalom, tricks, and jumping that survive in modern competition. Under AWSA's sponsorship, the national championships have been held every year since then, except during World War II.

During the War the first impromptu water ski show for visiting servicemen took place at Cypress Gardens, Florida. Through these shows—which later became a four-times-a-day routine—and the public relations wizardry of Dick Pope, Sr., more people have been introduced to the color and excitement of water skiing than by any other means.

The development of affordable, higher-horsepower outboard motors after World War II put the sport within the means of middle-class Americans for the first time (Figure 1.3). With the country finally out of the Depression, people had more money to spend on leisure activities, and participation in the sport soared.

International water ski competition got its start in 1946 when the French, Belgian, and Swiss water ski federations created the International Water Ski Union (IWSU). Joined by the United States the following year, the IWSU organized the first World Water Ski Championship at Juan-les-Pins, France in 1949. The tournament was won by the United States, which has dominated the team competition ever since, although numerous individual events have been won by skiers from Europe, Canada, and Australia. Many nations are now members of this international governing body which changed its name to the World Water Ski Union (WWSU) in 1955.

Figure 1.3. The availability of more powerful outboard motors, like this one at Cypress Gardens in 1951, signaled booming growth for the sport during the post-war era. Photo courtesy of Mercury Marine. Printed with permission.

After getting its start from Hains and other volunteer boosters, the American Water Ski Association was managed by the Outboard Boating Club of America for a number of years until establishing its own head-quarters in Winter Haven, Florida in 1958 and hiring William D. Clifford as its first executive manager. Under Clifford's long tenure, tournament skiing and club activity grew substantially.

Due to the efforts and vision of these pioneers and many others like them, water skiing today offers some of the most diverse recreational and competitive opportunities of any leisure activity.

A Diversity of Types

From the time Ralph Samuelson first rode his huge planks, people have been inventing new ways to have fun, to compete against each other, and to entertain onlookers on water skis. Consequently today there are many types of water skiing: everything from skiing without skis to skiing without a boat!

Recreational skiers are no longer restricted to two square-backed boards, although many people prefer a leisurely ride on two skis. For many others the joy and freedom of water skiing is epitomized by throwing up a wall of spray on a slalom ski. Still others like to ride "water toys." Not water skis in the traditional sense, these include kneeboards (Figure 1.4), discs, mini-surfboards, and inflatable tubes, sleds, and similar devices that can be towed behind powerboats.

Regardless of what they ride on, skiers need not be alone behind the boat. Skiing together with other people is a good way to share the fun. For those who are looking for something a bit more challenging, they can try doing turnarounds on stubby, rudderless trick skis or, for a faster pace, try barefooting with no skis at all (Figure 1.5).

Water skiing also has its serious, competitive forms. Each year water ski tournaments attract thousands of hard-core enthusiasts. The three events of regular AWSA-sanctioned water ski competition are slalom, tricks, and jumping. (A parallel system of competition has also been developed for barefoot skiing.) Like different pieces of apparatus in gymnastics, each event is a unique experience that appeals to a different facet of a competitor's personality. In slalom the skier becomes a racer, zipping back and forth through the zigzag slalom course (Figure 1.6).

Figure 1.4. Kneeboards have become very popular.

Figure 1.5. Barefooting is the ultimate challenge for many skiers.

Figure 1.6. Slalom emphasizes fluid motion and timing. Photo courtesy of Tom King. Printed with permission.

In tricks the skier is a dancer, skipping and twirling through a finely tuned program of maneuvers (Figure 1.7). In jumping the skier is a daredevil, hurling toward the jump ramp and then arcing through the air in a breathtaking leap (Figure 1.8).

Show skiing is yet another world within the galaxy of water skiing. The one type of skiing that is truly a group activity, shows are staged by amateur water ski clubs as well as professional troupes ã la Cypress Gardens. The best amateur clubs also compete against each other in water ski show tournaments. As pure entertainment, show skiing dresses up and adds a dash of sparkle to the standard types of water skiing and includes some types of its own, such as multi-tiered human pyramids (Figure 1.9), zany clown routines, graceful swivel ski acts, and colorful ballet lines. An outgrowth of show skiing is competitive freestyle skiing. In freestyle, which is best described as trick jumping, the contestants perform spectacular long distance flips, gainers, and other tricks off the jump ramp.

Figure 1.7. Trick skiing is like dancing on water. Photo courtesy of Tom King. Printed with permission.

Figure 1.8. Jumping is thrilling to skiers and spectators alike. Photo courtesy of Tom King. Printed with permission.

Figure 1.9. The human pyramid, a crowd-pleasing show act. Photo courtesy of Tom King. Printed with permission.

Water ski racing is the least known type of skiing in the United States, being confined mostly to the West Coast. Both circuit and marathon races (Figure 1.10) are held and every two years a World Water Ski Racing Championship takes place. A handful of thrill seekers also engage in drag racing—skiing quarter-mile runs against the clock on specially designed skis, or even barefooted behind powerful drag hydroplanes, sometimes at more than 100 miles per hour.

Then there is cable skiing: water skiing without a boat. Some years ago a West German engineer named Bruno Rixen developed the first commercially successful system for towing water skiers by means of an overhead cable. Now such systems are in operation throughout Europe and more are being built in the United States. Held aloft by steel towers and powered by an electric motor, the cable runs on pulleys in a continuous loop (Figure 1.11). When the skier is ready to start, the operator throws a lever that engages the end of the towrope to a carrier on the moving cable, and the skier is pulled gently from the dock. Depending on the size of the installation, 6, 8, 10, or more skiers can be pulled simultaneously.

As you can see, the sport of water skiing takes many forms. Each form is a unique and wonderful way to experience the thrill of skimming over the water. It's all there for you to discover.

Figure 1.10. A marathon water ski racer. Photo courtesy of Tom King. Printed with permission.

Figure 1.11. Boatless water skiing on a cableway. Photo courtesy of Tom King. Printed with permission.

CHAPTER 2

GEAR FOR THE WATER-SKIER

It is essential that you have good quality, properly fitting water ski equipment. Examine your needs carefully and try to base your equipment choices on value rather than emotion. As with many consumer goods, it often pays to spend a little more to get a better product; however, price alone is not an absolute test. You must avoid paying a lot of money for equipment that does not match your skill level or that is not designed for the intended use.

Selecting Water Skis

The quality of water skis has improved markedly in recent decades. There have been many improvements in design, but the primary advance has been in the materials used. Most water skis today are made of fiberglass formed around aluminum honeycomb or plastic foam cores. Some also have aluminum tops or rubber edges. Skis made of these space-age materials are lighter, faster, more maneuverable, easier to care for, and longer lasting than their wooden counterparts. In spite of this, quality wood skis can be an excellent value for the recreational skier because they are less expensive and with a little care will last a long time.

Although you may come across some bargain-basement skis of dubious quality, most skis manufactured today are made to high standards. This does not mean that you can buy anything on the rack and get what you want. You first have to carefully examine your needs to determine what type of ski(s) you need before deciding on a particular model.

Answers to these questions will help you focus on the type of skis to buy:

- Are you going to be the only one to use the skis or will they be shared by others?
- What is your weight? (Have you reached full size or are you still growing?)
- What is your skill level? (Beginner, recreational, advanced recreational, beginning tournament, advanced tournament.)
- Will the skis be used for recreation or competition, or both?
- How much money do you plan to spend?

Types of Skis

There are four basic types of water skis: standard and combination pairs, slaloms, trick skis, and jumpers. These can be further sorted into three price/performance categories: basic recreational, intermediate, and tournament. In addition, there are many types of novelty and training devices on the market.

Standard Pairs and Combination Pairs

The conventional square-backed water skis popular in the 1950s and 1960s have now been largely replaced by the more tapered combination pairs (combos) that have one ski set up with double binders so that it can be used as a single slalom. Equipped with adjustable binders, combos are the most versatile type of skis for family use (Figure 2.1). They have fairly wide tails and bottom designs that make them easy to get up on and comfortable to ride.

Both fiberglass and wood combo pairs are available. The main advantage of the fiberglass skis is their durability. If they are not abused, they will last practically forever with little or no maintenance. Don't ignore good quality wood combos, however, because they are less costly than glass skis and will last a long time if properly cared for.

The binders are generally a good indicator of the overall quality of the skis. Look for sturdy binder material that will provide support and that will not be likely to tear. Most quality binders are made of neoprene rubber or neoprene compounds. Avoid vinyl, which is hard and

Figure 2.1. Combination pairs are the most versatile for family use.

tears easily. The adjustment mechanism on adjustable binders should be simple and easy to operate (Figure 2.2). The thumb-screw type of adjustment, for example, is one that eliminates the need for any springs or catches that could eventually break. (Be careful not to tighten thumb screws too tightly—it's possible to pull them right out of the ski.) Most combo pairs come in a 67- to 68-inch length that is suitable for most adults. A few manufacturers also make junior combos that are about 10 inches shorter.

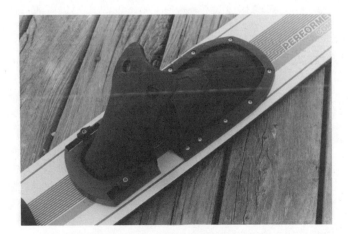

Figure 2.2. Binders should be adjustable to a snug fit.

Slaloms

There are many different models of slalom skis on the market. The choice of a particular ski will depend largely on your skill level. If you are just learning how to ride a single ski, or if you prefer a leisurely ride without any drastic cuts or turns, you will want a recreational-grade ski of fiberglass or wood that has a wide tail and a flat or nearly flat bottom. Such a ski will be easy to get up on and will track easily when ridden straight ahead.

As your ability increases and you begin making sharper turns and harder cuts, you will discover that this type of ski tends to skip out from under you in the turns. At this point you will probably want to graduate to a fiberglass intermediate-grade slalom that has a more tapered tail, beveled bottom edges, and a modified concave or tunnel concave bottom (Figure 2.3). A wide, flat-bottomed, square-edged ski rides high and fast, making turns difficult. A narrower tail allows the ski to ride deeper in the water, and the beveled edges help it to slow down so that a controlled turn can be made. The performance of a slalom ski can be changed by varying the amount of edge bevel in the front, midsection, and tail of the ski. Intermediate slaloms are designed to allow the advanced recreational or beginning competition skier to make sharp turns and still preserve the tame manners of recreational models.

Figure 2.3. A fiberglass intermediate-grade slalom ski.

A concave bottom helps the ski hold in turns by cupping the water. There are three major types. An edge-to-edge concave is one that extends across the entire width of the ski. A tunnel concave is narrower and creates a tunnel down the center of the ski with a flat surface on either side. A compound-radius concave is a variation of the edge-to-edge design with steeper edge "rails" (Figure 2.4).

Most intermediate-grade slaloms come in three or four lengths. Check the manufacturer's recommendations for the ski you should use for your weight. Although there is no absolute rule, normally skiers 125 pounds or less should consider a ski up to 64 inches long, skiers between 125 and 175 pounds a 66-inch ski, and skiers over 175 pounds a 68-inch or longer ski. Some manufacturers make scaled-down junior slaloms, with the same design features as the adult models, that range from 57 to 62 inches long.

Tournament-grade slaloms are designed with one limited purpose in mind: to help the "short-line" skier negotiate as many buoys in the slalom course as possible. These skis can turn sharply and accelerate and decelerate very quickly, but because they are more difficult to get up on and tend to wobble when ridden straight ahead, they are not recommended for recreational use. (They are also more expensive.) Tournament models have binders that are fixed to the skier's foot size and many have double "high wrap" straps that crisscross the ankle

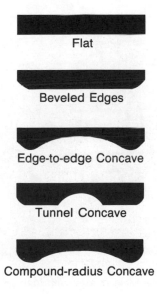

Flat

Beveled Edges

Edge-to-edge Concave

Tunnel Concave

Compound-radius Concave

Figure 2.4. Cross-sections show typical bottom shapes of slalom skis.

for greater support and control (Figure 2.5). Tournament-style binders are often mounted on a removable aluminum or plastic plate. Many competition skiers also mount heels on their rear binders to prevent their feet from coming out during slalom runs.

These top-of-the-line skis may contain exotic materials such as carbon graphite, Kevlar, boron, or titanium for strength and to achieve subtle flex and shock-dampening characteristics. Some are edge-to-edge concaves, others are tunnel concaves, while still others are compound-radius concaves. The variable-edge bevel on these skis helps them decelerate as the skier leans into the buoy yet accelerate easily after the turn.

Another device that has been employed to help the ski accelerate and decelerate quickly is fin wings. Resembling the wings of a jet fighter, these protrude from the fin at a critical angle. The wings create drag as the skier begins to turn, slowing down the ski like a brake; but when the skier leans back to pull, the wings become parallel to the flow of water and offer no resistance to acceleration (Figure 2.6). Fin wings are designed solely for short-line tournament use and would be a waste of money on a ski used only for recreation.

Figure 2.5. Tournament-type plate binder with high wrap straps.

Figure 2.6. Wings mounted on a slalom ski fin.

Tournament model slaloms also come in different lengths, including junior sizes. When shopping for any slalom ski, try to borrow the model ski you are thinking of buying to try it out first. Specialty ski shops and some marine dealers may have demonstrators to use. Keep in mind, however, that any new ski may take some time to get used to.

Trick Skis

Short, wide, blunt-ended, and finless, trick skis can turn and slide in any direction, allowing an amazing variety of tricks to be performed. Almost all are now made of fiberglass. The less expensive intermediate models are sold in pairs and come with adjustable binders (Figure 2.7). The tournament models are normally sold as single blanks (without binders), so that the user can mount a custom binder and a rear toe piece. The rear toe binder on a single trick ski is usually mounted at an angle in order to concentrate the weight in the center of the ski and to allow greater control of the ski's rotation.

Quality trick skis have beveled top sides that taper to a thin, crisp edge at the bottom. This design permits the ski to turn without resistance and prevents the edges from catching. Some trick skis have small grooves on the bottom to aid in tracking when skiing forward or backward. Tip shapes on trick skies vary from round to elliptical to nearly

Figure 2.7. Stubby trick skis have no fins.

square. The shape of the tip will not matter all that much to a beginning or intermediate trick skier.

Most intermediate-grade trick skis come in a 42-inch length suitable for an average-sized adult. Tournament models range from 40 to 44 inches for lighter or heavier skiers.

Jumpers

Jump skis may look like conventional square-backed recreational skis, but they are really the ultimate in modern water ski construction. Jumpers must be light and fast but incredibly strong to withstand the tremendous impact of long distance jump landings (Figure 2.8). Because of the quality that is needed, and because there is a limited demand for them, good jumpers are the most expensive type of skis made.

Most jump skis have aluminum honeycomb cores and fiberglass skins reinforced with carbon graphite fibers. Jump skis have short fins made of high-impact plastic and have plate-mounted binders. Different sizes, widths, and tapers are available to suit the individual taste of tournament jumpers.

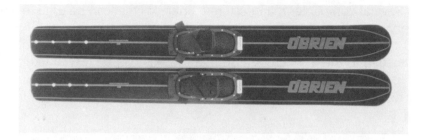

Figure 2.8. Jumpers must be extra strong. Photo courtesy of O'Brien International. Printed with permission.

Novelty Skis and Trainers

Besides the four basic types of water skis, there are a number of novelty devices on the market, including the popular kneeboards (Figure 2.9) as well as various sorts of rigid or inflatable rafts, sleds, and donut-shaped tubes. Each year some new toy comes on the market, so there is never an end to the variety of ways you can have fun on the water behind a boat.

Figure 2.9. Kneeboard has padded top and adjustable knee strap.

Several companies manufacture trainer skis that can be used to teach very young children how to water ski. The trainers consist of a pair of tot-sized skis that are tied together. The towrope and handle are attached to the front crosstie so that the skis can be towed like a sled (Figure 2.10). The trainers can be pulled behind a boat or by hand along a beach.

Figure 2.10. Trainer skis are tied together, towed like a sled. Photo courtesy of Casad Manufacturing Corp. Printed with permission.

Towropes and Handles

The standard water ski towrope is 75 feet long and has a single 12-inch handle. (Double-handled ski ropes are holdovers from a bygone era and are not recommended for proper skill development.) Recreational grade towropes are constructed of either polyethylene or polypropylene and are equipped with wooden handles or handles of aluminum tubing covered with soft foam. Competition-grade towropes are made of 12-strand polypropylene that meets or exceeds the AWSA tournament specification minimum breaking load of 1300 pounds. They have stronger aluminum-core handles with more durable molded or glued-on rubber compound grips. The better handles also have hand protectors—stiffeners where the rope joins the handle—to prevent chafing and, more importantly, to prevent the rope from accidentally looping around a finger (Figure 2.11). The hand protector usually consists of a short piece of vinyl tubing over the rope or is part of the molded grip of the handle.

A rope used for jumping looks much like a standard recreational rope, but slalom ropes have seven or eight take-off loops spliced at intervals into the main rope so that the rope can be shortened quickly after each

Figure 2.11. Towrope with molded hand protectors on handle. Photo courtesy of Casad Manufacturing Corp. Printed with permission.

"short-line" pass through the slalom course. Trick ropes are much shorter than conventional ropes, usually around 45 feet, and might have several take-off loops so that the skier can adjust the rope length to find the sharpest wake at the desired tricking speed. Trick ropes are often made of polyethylene, which sets after the first several times it is used and has less recoil than polypropylene.

Trick handle attachments, also called toehold harnesses, have a strap into which the free foot is inserted for performing "toehold" tricks. The strap, which is usually padded, must be properly sized to the foot because one that is too small might not come off readily in a fall (Figure 2.12).

One important safety device used by advanced trick skiers is the quick release. This is a mechanism mounted on the towing pylon that can release the towrope from the boat when it is tripped by the observer (Figure 2.13). Such a release is necessary when performing advanced reverse toehold tricks and other tricks in which there is a danger of the skier becoming entangled in the rope in a fall. While you may wish to consider using a quick release as an added safety measure when doing simple tricks, *do not rely on it*. A release is only as good as the person operating it, and it takes practice and experience to become a good release operator.

Figure 2.12. Trick attachment has padded toehold strap.

Figure 2.13. Removable towrope quick release mounted on pylon. Photo courtesy of Casad Manufacturing Corp. Printed with permission.

Ski Vests

Fortunately, the personal flotation devices (PFDs) available to water-skiers today have come a long way from the kapok-filled "horsecollars" and flimsy ski belts of yesteryear. A modern ski vest not only contains more flotation and is superior in terms of impact protection, but it is more comfortable and stylish and less restrictive of movement (Figure 2.14).

As a general rule you should always wear a Coast Guard–approved (Type III, wearable) ski vest when water skiing or kneeboarding. These vests are made of closed-cell foam (Ensolite) dipped in vinyl or covered with nylon fabric. Both types are excellent, although the vinyl ones tend to crack eventually at the shoulders. The best models have at least three nylon web straps going completely around the chest with strong plastic buckles. Make certain that the vest you purchase can be adjusted to a snug fit. If the vest rides up under your armpits when you are in the water, it is probably too big for you. If the vest doesn't meet in front when you pull the straps tight, it is too small for you.

Figure 2.14. Modern ski vests are comfortable and stylish.

Trick skiers often find the typical ski vests to be too restrictive when they are performing some of the more complicated tricks. For this reason trickers are not required to wear flotation devices in sanctioned tournaments where safety boats are always at the ready. Beginning trick skiers should wear ski vests and advanced trickers should wear some sort of flotation, such as a shorty wetsuit, when practicing. Check the regulations that apply where you ski.

Wetsuits and Drysuits

You can extend your skiing season earlier in the spring and later in the fall by wearing a wetsuit or drysuit. Wetsuits are made of buoyant, sponge-like neoprene foam that becomes saturated and allows a thin film of water next to the body that the body heats. With a full-length wetsuit you can still ski even when the water is quite cold.

Although scuba divers' wetsuits can be used, they tend to be bulky and heavy. A better choice is one of the lighter, more flexible suits designed specifically for water skiing (Figure 2.15). The best are lined with nylon on both sides, making them stronger and easier to put on and take off. Wetsuit gloves, booties, and hoods are also available for cold weather wear.

Shorty wetsuits, with short legs and sleeves, are popular with water-skiers because they keep the torso warm on chilly days yet allow free arm and leg movement. Wetsuits that incorporate long or short pants can provide valuable protection from painful injury to delicate body parts caused by the impact of water at high speeds. Both males and females should wear wetsuit pants or sturdy cloth shorts over the swimsuit when barefooting or jumping.

Special barefoot wetsuits are available that have additional thicknesses of neoprene on the back, chest, and rump for extra impact protection and flotation (Figure 2.16). (This extra foam also eliminates the need to wear a ski vest under the wetsuit.) These suits, invented in Australia, usually have short legs with cinch straps to prevent water from being forced into the suit during deepwater barefoot starts, tumbleturns, or other maneuvers. They come in long-sleeved, short-sleeved, or sleeveless styles. Once again, check the regulations where you ski before using a suit of this type in lieu of a ski vest.

A drysuit is just that. With seals at the neck, wrists, and ankles, this type of suit, made of rubberized fabric, does not allow water to enter

Figure 2.15. Full wetsuit can extend your skiing season. Photo courtesy of Casad Manufacturing Corp. Printed with permission.

Figure 2.16. Barefoot wetsuit has extra padding, cinch straps on legs.

(Figure 2.17). Additional insulation can be gained by wearing warm clothes like a sweatsuit or warmup suit underneath. Some skiers prefer drysuits because they feel less clammy than wetsuits, but they are also more expensive. Always wear a ski vest under or over a wetsuit (except a barefoot wetsuit) or drysuit.

Figure 2.17. Drysuit keeps body warm and dry. Photo courtesy of Casad Manufacturing Corp. Printed with permission.

Ski Gloves

Water ski gloves, widely used by slalom skiers, jumpers, and bare-footers, can help improve your grip and lessen fatigue at higher skiing speeds. The standard gloves are made of vinyl-impregnated fabric and usually have nylon mesh backs and adjustable wrist straps. These will usually last for only about a season of normal recreational use, less if used more frequently or for competition. The more expensive gloves are made of sturdier suede-like material, have heavier elastic on the backs, and have thicker straps (Figure 2.18).

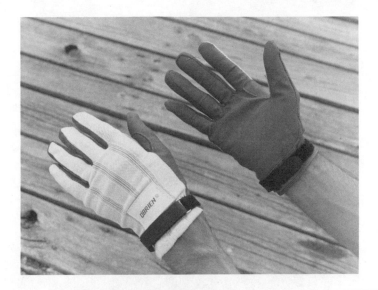

Figure 2.18. Ski gloves improve grip and lessen fatigue.

Care of Equipment

Here are some pointers to help keep your skis and other equipment in good condition:

- Keep equipment clean and dry. Rinse off any sand or dirt after use and put equipment where it can air dry.
- Keep equipment out of gasoline and oil. Don't let it get kicked around in the bottom of the boat.
- Protect skis from scratches by using a piece of carpet or other soft material on the dock. Never stand directly over the fin of a ski on a dock or you may damage the fin or split the ski.
- Store equipment out of direct sunlight in a well-ventilated area that does not get excessively hot, cold, or damp.
- Store skis flat on a rack or standing upright, not on top of one another.
- Store ski vests and wetsuits on wide clothes hangers, not in a pile.
- Coil ski ropes neatly without twists after every use and allow to dry. Untie any knots in a towrope before they get pulled tight or they will be difficult to get out (Figure 2.19).

Figure 2.19. Coil towrope neatly after use.

- Keep equipment in good repair. Fix dents in skis with epoxy and replace worn out or broken binders, hardware, and fins. Discontinue using ropes if they are frayed. Do not use ski vests that are torn or have broken straps or buckles.

A Word About Boats

Just about every type of motorized watercraft—from small fishing boats to huge diesel-powered express ferry boats—has been used to tow water-skiers. Just because a boat can tow skiers, however, doesn't mean that it's a good ski boat for recreational use. When selecting a boat for water skiing, here are some important characteristics to look for.

Hull Type and Power

Runabouts in the 15- to 25-foot range are usually favored for water skiing. Smaller boats can be used for light-duty towing, such as for very young skiers or kneeboarders, but they tend to handle poorly or lack power when towing adults on skis. Boats larger than 25 feet can be cumbersome to maneuver at slow speeds and often have high sides, cabins, or other features that restrict the driver's visibility. Most family runabouts in the recommended size range are now made of gel-coated fiberglass or aluminum that needs little maintenance compared to wood.

Outboard, inboard, or stern-drive boats can make excellent towing rigs. Regardless of the type of propulsion, the horsepower needed will depend on the weight and skill of the skiers and the type of skiing they do. Motors of less than 50 horsepower may be adequate for pulling youngsters, kneeboarders, or beginning trick skiers, but for pulling adults from deepwater starts on one or two skis, hard-pulling teenagers, multiple skiers, and so forth, 75 horsepower or more will probably be needed. The more advanced types of skiing, such as serious barefooting and competition slalom, will require even more power, generally at least 150 horsepower. The powerplant must be matched to the size and type of boat and must not exceed the boat's maximum horsepower rating.

Regardless of its rated horsepower, the motor must be set up properly and have the right propeller to be useful for towing skiers. Even a 200-horse outboard that is mounted too high on the transom or swinging a prop that is the wrong pitch can be worthless for pulling an average-sized adult from a deepwater start. The pitch of the propeller refers to the angle of the blades. Consult your marine dealer for specific recommendations on how to set up your motor and select the right propeller for towing water-skiers.

Handling

A ski boat should plane quickly when the throttle is advanced. Once on plane, it should be able to maintain a straight path and not roll drastically or wander when a skier cuts out hard to one side. The driver should not have to fight the wheel to keep the boat on track. The boat should also corner without heeling over excessively. Maneuverability at low speed is important, too, because of the need to operate close to skiers in the water.

Wakes

Skiers, particularly young ones, can have great difficulty skiing behind a boat that throws a gigantic wake. Trick skiers and kneeboarders like to have a moderate sized wake to jump at 13 to 18 miles per hour, and slalom skiers appreciate a small wake at speeds above 25 miles per hour. The table—the area between the wakes where the skier rides—should be free of excessive turbulence, deep troughs, or rooster tails.

Visibility

Good visibility for the driver is a must. The deck should not be cluttered with too many railings, flag poles, spot lights, or other hardware that can get in the way. Some types of windshields can hamper visibility, especially if the top of the bracket is at eye level. High sides on some boats can make it difficult to see when maneuvering around a downed skier. While the bow of most boats will rise somewhat during acceleration, some rise too high or stay up for too long before planing.

Controls

A water ski boat must be responsive. The steering and throttle action must be smooth and positive without too much play. The throttle should be positioned so that the driver can reach it while sitting comfortably erect. Ideally there should be a support for the driver's forearm to help prevent fatigue and to allow for fine speed adjustments to be made with the wrist and fingers rather than the entire arm. (A foot throttle is generally not recommended.) The gear shift should be of single-lever design and it should shift crisply without hesitation or stalling.

Seating

The driver should be seated comfortably where he or she has good visibility and can reach the controls without having to lean forward from the seat back. The observer should be able to face the skier without craning the neck. Tournament ski boats have rear-facing observer/judges seats. In a bowrider boat, make sure that the forward passengers can be seated so that they will not block the driver's view.

Interior Room and Storage

A good ski boat will have lots of room for skiers to get their gear ready and to allow the observer to move about freely when picking up skis, reeling in the towrope, or helping skiers get in the boat (Figure 2.20). Storage space for skis, ropes, and vests under the deck, gunwales, or seats is not only a convenience but also reduces clutter that could cause a fall.

Figure 2.20. A fully-rigged outboard ski boat with central pylon and rear-facing observer's seat.

Boarding

The boat should be easy to get into from the water. An inexpensive portable boarding ladder may be all that is needed. Some boats have steps or fold-down ladders and assist handles built-in. A transom-mounted swim platform is a highly desirable accessory that makes boarding easy and allows the skier to drip off before getting into the boat.

Tow Pylon

It is best to attach the towrope to a towing pylon (a special post or tripod mounted inside the boat). Use of a pylon has several advantages over simply tying the rope to the transom or using a pulley-type harness across the stern. Because it is farther forward, closer to the boat's turning axis, the pylon helps the boat to track straight. It also holds the rope high enough to keep it from dragging through the wake, which is a great help to the skier, and allows the driver to maneuver more easily at idle speed without fear of fouling the towrope in the propeller. Because the observer does not have to lean over the transom to reach it, retrieving or untangling the towrope is also much easier and safer.

Most boats that are designed for serious skiing include pylons as standard equipment. There are also several types of pylons available as bolt-on accessories. Be sure to follow the manufacturer's installation instructions carefully. A pylon that is too high can alter the handling characteristics of the boat when a skier pulls out hard to one side. Passengers should always be seated forward of the pylon when it is in use.

Rear View Mirror

Although the driver should rely primarily on the observer to keep tabs on the skier, a good rear view mirror is a valuable asset. A mirror allows the driver to maintain a forward lookout while monitoring the location of the skier. The large, flat, truck-type mirrors, such as the one shown in Figure 2.21, are the best. The smaller curved mirrors available at most marine dealers distort the image, which may make it difficult to make out the skier's hand signals, but even one of these is preferable to no mirror at all.

Figure 2.21. Well-laid-out cockpit shows mirror, dual speedometers and other instrumentation, throttle handle position, and adjustable driver's seat.

Speedometer

A good driver strives to hold a constant speed. Even a half-mile-per-hour variance can affect the skier. Holding an accurate speed can only be done with the aid of a speedometer.

Most boat speedometers measure the pressure of the water as the boat moves through it. A device called a pitot tube extends into the water at the transom. Water is forced into the tube with increasing pressure as the boat moves faster. This in turn increases air pressure in a small plastic hose, which moves the needle on the speedometer dial. Because of the effect of currents and the possibility that the mechanism may need to be calibrated, speedometer readings should not be taken as absolute unless they are confirmed by timing the boat with a stopwatch over a known distance. Regardless of this, boat speedometers are indispensable for gauging relative changes in speed. Speedometers are frequently installed on new boats; they can also be purchased from marine dealers and are easy to mount.

CHAPTER 3

IT'S SAFE BUT . . .

Untold numbers of people have water-skied for years without ever suffering serious injury. Yet each summer there are sensational headlines about people who have been killed or maimed in water skiing accidents. Just how safe is the sport?

Water skiing is safe, but like many strenuous recreational activities, it is safe only if precautions are followed. If you ride a bicycle and ignore traffic signals, or if you go ice skating and don't check the thickness of the ice, you are asking for trouble. It's the same with water skiing. There are rules that you must not violate, or sooner or later you're going to get hurt. Most serious water skiing accidents are the result of someone having disregarded one or more of the basic safety rules.

The Ten Commandments of Safe Water Skiing

By exercising common sense and following these recommended safety guidelines, you too can have decades of safe skiing fun (Figure 3.1).

1. *Know how to swim, and wear a flotation device at all times.* For most skiing a Coast Guard–approved Type III PFD that is designed for water skiing is ideal. Your ski vest must fit snugly. A loose-fitting vest can come off in a hard fall. Avoid ski belts, since they offer little flotation and no impact-protection for the rib cage. Specialty wetsuits that offer both flotation and impact-protection are available for certain advanced types of skiing such as barefooting. (Note: Flotation devices are not required of contestants in trick skiing events in AWSA-sanctioned tournaments due to the slow speed and the immediate presence of safety boats. While

Figure 3.1.   Safe skiing means following a few simple rules.

Type III devices are sometimes too cumbersome for the more advanced trick maneuvers, always wear some sort of flotation, such as a shorty wetsuit, when practicing tricks.) Check your state's boating regulations for skier flotation requirements.

2. *Know and use the proper hand and voice signals.* These are explained in the next section.
3. *Ski only in suitable waters that you and your driver are familiar with.* This means avoiding areas that are too small, too shallow, too obstructed, or too crowded with other boat traffic. The water should be at least 5 feet deep. Use good judgment in determining the amount of surface area you will need for the type of skiing you will be doing. Give yourself plenty of room to maneuver. Do not ski near swimming beaches, marinas, boat mooring areas, or busy navigation channels. Stay away from ships or barges that cannot maneuver to avoid you.
4. *Use equipment that is properly sized and in good repair.* Your skis should be the right size. Bindings, vests, gloves, and so forth should fit snugly. Inspect your equipment before use. Don't use

frayed towropes, vests with broken straps or buckles, or skis with cracks, sharp edges, torn binders, or loose or broken hardware.

5. *Ski only behind competent towboat drivers*. A good boat driver is your best safety device. Don't ski behind anyone whose judgment or ability you distrust.

6. *Stay clear of shore, docks, pilings, other boats, and other solid objects*. Some of the most serious water ski injuries result from collisions with the shore or with structures on or in the water. This is a pity because such accidents are almost always avoidable. Watch where you are going. Don't show off by attempting to land near docks or floats or by skiing up on shore. It's easy to misjudge your speed and come in too fast.

7. *Respect the towrope*. The power of the towboat is concentrated in the towrope. It can cause severe injury if it is not respected. Hold the handle, not the rope, when skiing. Never wrap the towrope around any part of your body, and never place the handle over your head. When preparing for a start, always hold the rope as if the boat is going to accelerate without warning. Never wear a ring when skiing because it might catch on the handle or the rope. Never ski over or attempt to pick up a loose towrope when skiing double.

8. *Do not ski at night, when visibility is poor, or when dangerous weather conditions exist*. Don't ski when it is raining or foggy, and get off the water at the first approach of an electrical storm.

9. *Know your limitations*. Don't attempt maneuvers beyond your ability. Ski in control. Work on new skills gradually. Never ski to the point of exhaustion.

10. *Do not ski (or allow your driver to drive) while under the influence of alcohol or drugs*. Things happen quickly when you are water skiing, and you must be alert and ready to react without impairment. It is a dangerous mistake to think that it's OK to bring along a six-pack in the boat when you go skiing.

Hand and Voice Signals

The skier, the boat driver, and the observer must be able to communicate clearly. Over the years skiers have developed a number of voice commands and hand signals that are universally recognized. Make sure that you and your driver and observer know them well.

You can use verbal commands while getting ready to ski. For instance, when you have your skis on and you want the boat to idle forward slowly, you should say "In gear" or "Take up slack." (Don't say "OK" or "Ready" because your driver may accelerate the boat, thinking that you are ready to take off.) When the slack has been taken up and you are in position and ready to ski, your command should be "Hit it." If you are not in position, or if the towrope becomes tangled and you want to stop the slack from being taken up, call "Neutral." (Don't say "Hold it," because that can easily and dangerously be confused with "Hit it." "No" can also sound like "Go.")

Use the following hand signals to communicate once you are up and skiing. If you want the boat to speed up, indicate by a "thumbs up" gesture (Figure 3.2); show "thumbs down" if you want the boat to go slower (Figure 3.3). Use the thumb-and-forefinger "OK" sign to tell the boat crew that the speed is correct (Figure 3.4).

Figure 3.2. Faster.

Figure 3.3. Slower.

Figure 3.4. Speed OK.

Want the boat to turn? Indicate this by making a circling motion with an up-pointed finger (Figure 3.5), then point in a wide arc to the right or the left if you want the boat to turn in a particular direction. These signals can also be used by the boat driver or observer to let you know that the boat is going to make a turn. The driver or observer can also warn you that rough water or boat wakes are ahead by making a wavy motion with the hand.

If you want the boat to slow down completely and drop you into the water, use the traffic police officer's signal for "stop" (Figure 3.6). When you want the boat to return to shore or to the dock, pat the top of your head (Figure 3.7). You can also pat your head after a fall to tell the boat crew that you want to be picked up in the boat. If you want to tell the driver to turn off the motor, draw an index finger across your windpipe in a cutting motion (Figure 3.8).

Figure 3.5. Turn.

Figure 3.6. Stop.

Figure 3.7. Back to dock.

Figure 3.8.   Cut motor.

After each and every fall, clasp both of your hands high over your head to tell the boat crew that you're not hurt. If they don't see this signal, they will assume that you are hurt and will rush back to your aid. Don't give them an unnecessary scare; always use the "skier OK" signal if you are unhurt after you fall (Figure 3.9).

Sometimes you will fall in an area where other boats are operating. To the other boat pilots you may be difficult to see, and they will probably not be expecting someone to be in the water so far from shore. To make yourself more visible, hold a ski vertically out of the water (Figure 3.10) and, if necessary, wave it back and forth. Your own tow-boat, of course, should return to you quickly after you have fallen.

Figure 3.9. Skier OK after fall.

Figure 3.10. Look out, skier in water.

Laws and Regulations

Each state has its own laws and regulations governing water skiing, and in some cases local governments and state or federal agencies may have special regulations on waterways under their jurisdiction. Be sure that you become familiar with all of the applicable laws where you ski. Although they vary from area to area, the most common types of regulations you should check for include:

- Flotation devices. Some states require that the skier wear a flotation device; some specify that it be a Coast Guard–approved device. In other states the skier does not have to wear a PFD, but there must be one in the boat for the skier.
- Observer vs. mirror. An observer may be required. Furthermore, the observer may have to be of a certain age. In some states an approved wide-angle rear view mirror may be used instead of an observer.
- Skiing hours. Most states prohibit water skiing during nighttime hours, but the official definition of when daylight begins and ends varies widely. A few local waterways may also be time zoned, where water skiing is permitted only during certain hours of the day.
- Safe separation. A "safe separation distance" is normally specified by state law. This is the distance that powerboats must remain away from shore, other boats, and fixed objects when moving fast. Generally this distance is 100 feet, but it may be greater. In some cases adherence to a designated boat traffic pattern may also be necessary.

There are many other sorts of laws and regulations. Remember, though, that all of them are designed for your safety and the safety of the others on the water. Know and obey them all.

Water Ski Etiquette

Regardless of the laws, regulations, ordinances, or rules that apply on the waterway where you ski, always be courteous toward others on the water (Figure 3.11) and respect the rights of waterfront landowners. Stay away from people fishing and people in canoes, sailboats, and other slow-moving craft. Give a wide berth to other skiers and powerboats. Use discretion as to how early in the morning you start skiing;

Figure 3.11. Be courteous to others when you water-ski.

your noise may bother others. Never attempt to spray people on shore, docks, or in other boats or engage in any other unsafe horseplay.

It is very unfortunate that only a few irresponsible skiers who do not respect the rights of others can sometimes sway public opinion against all water-skiers. More than one waterway has had restrictions or bans imposed on water skiing due to the antics of one or two bad apples. If you don't want to lose the privilege of being able to use your local lake or river for water skiing, be a good water ski citizen and encourage other skiers to do the same.

Physical Conditioning for Water Skiing

Water-skiers often say that they discover "new" muscles after they ski. The soreness and stiffness in unfamiliar places that can make it difficult to get out of bed the next morning result from using muscles that are rarely called into play in daily life. A person who is in poor condition runs a much greater risk of incurring muscle strains, sprained ligaments, and worse from overexertion and especially from awkward, twisting falls. Because of this it is important to be in good shape for water skiing. This is particularly true of older individuals, since the elasticity of body tissues declines with age.

If you are physically active and have reasonably good muscle tone, you should not have any problems (beyond some normal minor stiffness) from taking a leisurely ride on skis. However, as you advance in skill and attempt more difficult maneuvers, it is wise to begin a conditioning program that will help you avoid injury and improve your skiing performance.

A well-rounded conditioning program is aimed at doing three things: (a) enhancing muscle strength through gradually increasing the load or work performed, (b) increasing muscle flexibility through stretching, and (c) improving cardiovascular endurance through extended aerobic activity.

The best overall conditioning program for water skiing is water skiing. If you water-ski frequently (several times each week) and are careful to start slowly, and if you gradually increase the intensity of your skiing and the time you spend on the water, you are using the right muscle groups in precisely the right way and, aside from stretching, no further conditioning will be needed. However, few people are able to ski this much. If, like most skiers, you are able to ski only on occasional weekends, you may want to supplement your program with other fitness activities. This is especially important at the beginning of the skiing season. Activities like jogging, walking, and cycling (and ice skating and snow skiing, in the off-season) are good for keeping the legs in shape and maintaining aerobic capacity. Keeping the arms, shoulders, and back in shape for skiing is more difficult, since few other leisure activities involve pulling. Rowing, either in a boat or on a rowing machine, is about the best alternative for this purpose. Regardless of the activity, do it several times a week for at least 20 to 30 minutes each time for best results.

Weight training, with free weights or progressive-resistance machines, can also be beneficial. Top tournament skiers frequently work out with weights, especially in the off-season. Seek professional help before you begin a weight training program.

It is important to incorporate stretching exercises as part of any conditioning program. Tight, inflexible muscles are more prone to tearing and pulling injuries. Consult reliable sports and fitness sources for information on which stretching exercises to do and the proper technique to use.

Get in the habit of stretching and warming up each time before you water-ski. Spend a few minutes stretching and doing jumping jacks, running in place, or swimming vigorously to get the blood running and your muscles warm and limber. It is particularly important to warm up when the air or water is cold.

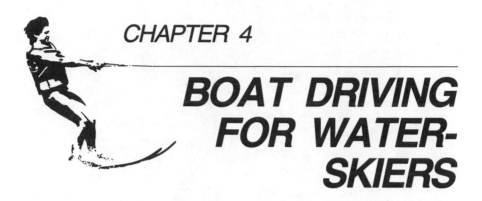

CHAPTER 4

BOAT DRIVING FOR WATER-SKIERS

Safe and enjoyable water skiing requires a team effort. The skier, the observer, and the driver must know and faithfully perform their duties. Under normal circumstances the skier can choose when to go, in what direction, and at what speed. The observer passes signals back and forth between the skier and the driver, notifies the driver if the skier has fallen, and looks for the "skier OK" signal after each fall. The observer also picks up skis, reels in the towrope, and helps the skier get into the boat. As the driver, however, you have the most important job. While you want to satisfy the skier, you are ultimately in command and must take whatever action is necessary to assure safety. Your responsibilities as a powerboat pilot, considerable to begin with, are increased when a skier is swinging from side to side behind your craft. Not only do you share a big part of the responsibility for the skier's safety, but how well you drive can have a big impact on the skier's performance and skill development (Figure 4.1).

Driving boats for water-skiers is fun and rewarding, but it takes special knowledge, the right attitude, and a good deal of practice to do well. Before towing any water-skiers, you must understand the principles of small boat handling and have considerable experience as a power-boat operator. Ideally, you should have attended a course in boating safety given by the U.S. Coast Guard Auxiliary, the U.S. Power Squadrons, the Red Cross, or your state boating safety education office. You must be aware of the applicable boating regulations for your locale

Figure 4.1. The boat driver is ultimately in command.

and know the skiers' hand and voice signals. You should also have gained a knowledge of what the skier wants and needs. This will be easier if you are a skier yourself; but even if you are not, you can learn by observing and talking to skiers.

The right attitude means being safety conscious at all times and having a desire to always give the skier the best ride possible. Good drivers understand that they are driving for the skier's benefit, not their own.

Boat driving for skiers is a skill and, like any skill, it takes practice and a willingness to improve. The best way to start out is to volunteer on a regular basis to be an observer for other water ski drivers whose ability you admire. Then when you feel you are ready, ask one of these experienced drivers to come along to supervise when you tow your first skiers. At first it's best to pull experienced skiers only because they will be better able than beginners to make up for your mistakes if your turns or starts are not perfect.

To be a good towboat driver, you have to develop a touch that requires a thorough understanding of how your actions at the wheel will affect your skier. It will take a lot of practice, but you'll get better at it as you gain experience.

Starts

Always take up slack very slowly and only when your skier tells you to do so. If the rope becomes tangled or if the skier gets out of position, put the motor in neutral immediately. When the skier has the handle, orient the boat so that the skier, the rope, and the boat are in a straight line for a direct pull and make sure that the motor or the rudder is pointed straight ahead, as shown in Figure 4.2.

Advance the throttle only when the skier yells "Hit it." Never accelerate just because you think the skier is ready—at best you may cause the

Figure 4.2. Skier should be directly behind boat before start.

skier to fall because he or she is not anticipating the pull; at worst you may not see the rope looped around an arm or a leg under water. Always check carefully in front of you before accelerating. The bow of most boats will rise when power is applied, and your view may be blocked momentarily.

Accelerate firmly and smoothly and work toward developing a feel for just the right amount of throttle to apply for the skier's weight and skill. Many new drivers accelerate too fast. It is rarely necessary to "floor it." On the other hand, if the skier does not have sufficient speed, the takeoff will be grueling. Seek a happy medium. Watch the skier in your mirror. If you must turn around to watch the start, have your observer look ahead for you until the skier is up and you can once again look forward.

Under Way

Strive to keep the desired speed as constant as possible. Sit erect with your back against the seat back. Keep constant pressure on the throttle handle with a fingers-and-wrist action. You should be able to look ahead and keep an eye on the speedometer and mirror without having to turn your head much.

Most beginning skiers will not know what speed they want. You'll have to watch a new skier closely to set an appropriate speed, one that is not so fast that he or she is skipping along with little control yet not so slow that the skis are bogging down and pushing a lot of water. Look to see how the skis are planing. Again, look for that happy medium. First-time drivers tend to go too fast. Lightweight youngsters may require as little as 10 to 15 miles per hour; most adults will be comfortable at between 20 and 25 miles per hour. The more experienced skiers will, of course, be able to signal the boat to set the speeds they desire. When your skier signals to go faster or slower, change speeds gradually.

Remember that it's your job to look ahead and steer a safe course. Don't get into the habit of constantly turning around and gawking at your skier; let the observer do that job. Do get in the habit of checking on the skier in the rear view mirror while looking where you are going. Always sit down while driving; never stand up or sit on the gunwale or the back of the seat.

Stay a safe distance from other boats, shore, pilings, docks, and other obstructions. The skier can swing out 75 feet to either side of the boat, so, as a rule of thumb, stay at least 100 feet from objects with which your skier could potentially collide. (Check your state's boating regulations for the minimum safe separation distance.) The exception to this is when making a shore landing.

Do not allow another boat to follow too closely behind you when you are pulling a skier. You cannot be sure that the operator of that boat will notice if your skier falls. If a boat trails you too closely, wave it away and take evasive action by turning to one side. You should always be able to return to your fallen skier before any other boat comes close.

Turns

Make all turns gradually and make sure you know where the skier is and that he or she knows of your intention before beginning to turn (Figure 4.3). If the skier is cutting out to one side and you turn in the opposite direction, centrifugal force will cause the skier to accelerate, perhaps to the point where control is lost. Avoid whipping your skier, even in fun. On the other hand, if you turn toward the skier, he or she will begin to lose speed and sink. The trick is to keep the *skier's* speed constant throughout the turn, which may require speeding up or slowing down the boat, depending on the circumstances.

Figure 4.3. Be aware of the position of the skier before turning.

Generally speaking, water-skiers want to ski in calm water. If you drive in a circle or in a random pattern, you will create rough water conditions for your skier by constantly recrossing your own wake. This may be fine for skiers who are just taking a leisurely ride, but if they are trying to learn a new skill or practicing a maneuver that requires calm water, use the barbell pattern. This involves making a straight run followed by a 180° buttonhook turn that brings you back in the opposite direction on the same path where your own wake has dissipated (Figure 4.4). All competition boat patterns are some variation of this barbell pattern.

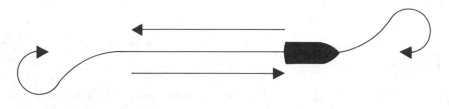

Figure 4.4. Barbell boat pattern.

Falls

If your skier falls, return without delay. This means that your observer must be attentive at all times and that you should check your mirror frequently. There is nothing quite so frustrating to skiers in the water than to watch their towboats go merrily down the lake with no one aware that they have fallen. With other boats operating in the area, a downed skier is vulnerable—so return quickly.

After a fall the observer should look for the "skier OK" sign. If there is no other boat traffic, you can cut the throttle and idle back while the skier recovers and puts on the skis. If other boats are nearby or if the skier does not give the OK sign and is presumed to be hurt, maintain speed and turn as quickly as you safely can and get back to the skier right away.

Approach a downed skier slowly and begin to circle from the driver's side for good visibility. Put the motor in neutral as you drift past. Be aware of and compensate for winds or currents that may push the boat into the skier. Once you are well past the skier, put the motor in gear and turn in the opposite direction. This will swing the stern so that the towrope comes within the skier's reach. Under normal circumstances a skier should not have to swim after the towrope. Practice until you can bring the rope to the skier every time. Figure 4.5 illustrates the procedure.

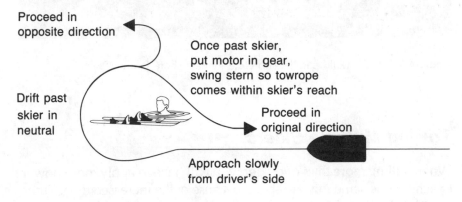

Proceed in
opposite direction

Once past skier,
put motor in gear,
swing stern so towrope
comes within skier's reach

Drift past
skier in
neutral

Proceed in
original direction

Approach slowly
from driver's side

Figure 4.5. Picking up a fallen skier.

Landings

Shore landings should be made only by skiers skilled enough to control their approaches and only into uncrowded areas where the bottom contours are known. Parallel the shore at a relatively slow speed and let your skier swing out and drop off. The skier should not attempt to ski too close to shore or docks but should drop off a safe distance out and swim in (Figure 4.6). Never whip a skier toward shore.

Do not land a skier into a crowded beach or dock area where other boats, skiers, and swimmers are congregated. It is much safer in such circumstances to drop off your skiers in open water and pick them up in the boat for the ride back to shore. Always turn off the motor before allowing a skier to climb into the boat.

After your skier has let go, idle down and have your observer bring in the towrope. Do not let a ski rope dangle behind the boat if it is not going to be used immediately.

Figure 4.6. Boat should parallel shoreline for safe shore landing.

Towing Multiple Skiers

When pulling more than one skier, you will have to apply more power to achieve the same forward speed because of the increased drag. Turns must be more gradual, and you will have to be aware of the positions of all your skiers. The feel will be entirely different from the feel when pulling a single skier, so you will have to keep a closer watch on the skiers to give them a good ride (Figure 4.7).

Figure 4.7. Pulling multiple skiers takes practice.

For safety, make certain that your skiers are all using equal-length ropes, and check the pylon or other ski rope attachment to make sure that you don't exceed its rated capacity.

When skiing multiple, your skiers should be instructed to let go immediately if any one of the other skiers falls. This way the group stays together and you will not have to maintain skiing speed during your return.

The skiers you pull work hard to learn. You owe it to them to work just as hard to be a good towboat driver. Above all, always keep in mind that you are driving for their benefit, not your own.

The Role of the Observer

If you act as an observer, take the job seriously because it's an important one. It's not difficult, and it can be a lot of fun; but you must pay attention, because the skier and the driver both need you.

Before the start you can help the skier get ready. It's best if the skier puts on the skis next to the boat where you can hand them over the side one by one. Tossing skis to a skier who is far from the boat can result in missing widely and forcing the skier to swim after them, or in hitting the skier in the face or on the head.

As the observer you are the towrope handler. The rope should be stored neatly coiled. If it isn't, take the time to recoil it to avoid tangles and knots when the boat takes up the slack. Ski ropes have attachment loops on the ends but it is not advisable to merely place this loose loop over the top of the pylon. Instead, feed the main part of the rope through the loop to form a secondary loop that, when placed over the pylon, will pull tight and not come off. With the rope neatly coiled and the end attached to the pylon, place the coils in the water and give the handle to the skier. Then sit down where you can face the skier comfortably and can easily relay signals to the driver. (If you are back by the motor, the driver may not be able to hear you.)

As the slack is taken up prior to the start, watch for tangles in the rope. If you see a tangle, tell the driver to put the motor in neutral and then reel in the rope to fix it. (The skier can do this if the tangle is near him or her.) Most tangles form from loops in the rope tightening around themselves. Pull the tangle apart to loosen it and pull the loops through.

It normally isn't necessary to pull the end of the rope through to unsnarl such a tangle.

Always let the skier give the signal to start. Never tell the driver to accelerate on a mere assumption that the skier is ready, because you may be wrong. If the driver must watch the skier's start, keep a forward lookout for other boat traffic until the skier is up and the driver can look forward.

Be attentive and watch the skier at all times. Relay any signals promptly to the driver. Do not distract the driver; he or she has a lot to do in steering a safe course and keeping a steady speed. Keep an eye out for other boats, and let the driver know of any that may be approaching too closely from the side or from the rear. If the skier drops a ski, note its approximate location so that you can find it easily later.

Notify the driver immediately if the skier falls, and look for the "skier OK" signal. Also, watch for other boats that may be approaching the fallen skier. With the cooperation of the driver, retrieve any skis that may have drifted too far for the skier to reach easily. If the skier wishes to get in the boat, get out the boarding ladder and help the skier board the boat. Coil the towrope neatly, and keep it from becoming tangled by tying the loop-end of the rope around the coils. Stow the towrope and skis where they will not be tripped over.

Always remain in your seat until the boat has slowed down and settled in the water before getting up to reach for skis in the water or to reel in the rope. It is easy to lose your balance and fall if the boat hits a wake or turns suddenly.

While it is beyond the scope of this book to teach water rescue techniques, one word of caution is appropriate. If skiers are ever injured and unable to get into the boat, do not drag them passively over the side; this could aggravate spinal injuries. Instead, victims should be supported on backboards and floated to shore where emergency medical help can be summoned.

CHAPTER 5

KNEE-BOARDING

Many different kinds of novelty skis and devices have been popular at one time or another over the years. The aquaplane was in use long before conventional water skis. Later, large plywood discs, stubby little shoe skis, miniature slalom skis, inflatable tubes and sleds, and other such devices captured the fancy of water-skiers seeking a different experience.

Today, although a number of high-tech water toys are on the market, the one that has had by far the biggest impact has been the kneeboard. Short, wide, and bullet-shaped with a padded top, a kneeboard is designed to be ridden in a kneeling position (Figure 5.1).

Figure 5.1. Kneeboarding is easy and fun.

The reasons for the kneeboard's popularity are not hard to find. Like aquaplanes and discs, kneeboards do not require a lot of speed or a lot of horsepower. With such a large planing area they can be enjoyed even behind boats powered by small fishing motors. Kneeboards, however, are much more versatile than their wooden predecessors. They can be used to cut hard, to jump wakes, and even to do turns and side-slides, and they can be ridden lying down, kneeling, sitting, or standing. As you will see in Chapter 12, they can even be used to learn how to barefoot.

Although designed for fun, kneeboards are also valuable tools for learning how to water-ski. They are easier to get up on and can help you experience what it is like to be towed behind a boat.

Boarding Basics

Kneeboards plane quickly and easily, although getting up on one does require some dexterity. The takeoff is accomplished by lying on top of the board with your legs trailing behind. Mount the board by grasping both sides, sinking the tail, and pulling it underneath you. Move as far forward as you can while still keeping the nose of the board up. Because the board floats like a cork, make sure that your weight is centered or the board will squirt out from under you.

Tell the driver to put the boat in gear, and guide the rope loosely through your fingers. When the slack has been taken up, prop yourself up on your elbows and grasp the handle with both hands up near the nose of the board. When getting up, you control the board with your elbows. When you are ready, tell the driver to "Hit it" and lean back a bit to keep the nose up (Figure 5.2a). The boat should accelerate very slowly. As the board begins to plane on top of the water, shift your weight forward to your elbows (Figure 5.2b).

Use a slow boat speed (10 to 14 miles per hour) at first for stability while getting to your knees. Without moving your elbows and forearms, draw your knees up under you (Figure 5.2c). Then sit up cautiously. If the nose of the board begins to bounce, your weight is too far back. Drop back down to your elbows, move your knees farther forward and try it again. If the board no longer bounces when you sit up, your weight is adequately positioned (Figure 5.2d).

a

b

Figure 5.2. Deepwater kneeboard start (cont. on next page).

c

d

Figure 5.2.   Deepwater kneeboard start (cont.).

On your first ride, don't use the knee strap. Just kneel on top of the strap until you get used to the board. Later you can strap in by letting go with one hand and holding the strap as you slide your knees under it. Most straps have a Velcro adjustment so that you can tighten it. (Don't pull it too tight.)

Cutting—moving from side to side behind the boat—is a simple matter of leaning while pulling the handle in toward the hip (the left hip if you are leaning to the right and vice versa). If you cut hard enough, you can cross over the boat's wake and cruise along outside.

When you have gained some experience maneuvering back and forth, you'll want to try jumping the wake. When you do, you will find that your board will bounce off the wake even on a mild cut. You can shorten the towrope to find the sharpest wake for jumping. When cutting on a kneeboard, your center of gravity is back toward the tail and when you hit the wake the nose of the board will tend to fly up, like a motorcycle doing a wheelie. For longer wake jumps, initiate the jump with your head and upper torso but keep the board level in the air, as shown in Figure 5.3, by controlling it with your knees. Caution: Keep the nose of the board up when you land. If it digs in, you will have a hard fall.

Figure 5.3. A kneeboard becomes airborne easily.

Kneeboards are somewhat less maneuverable than water skis, and they don't have brakes. Be extra careful that you are not near shore, other boats, or any solid objects before you go slipping and sliding along outside the wakes.

Kneeboard Start

1. Guide board with elbows.
2. When planing, draw knees under you and sit up.
3. Move forward if board bounces.

Turnarounds

Turnarounds are easier to perform on a kneeboard than on trick skis because you don't have to worry about keeping two skis together and your low center of gravity when kneeling makes exact body position less critical. You do have to use more "body English" to get the board around, and the handle pull must be exaggerated.

Start a front-to-back turn by leaning forward and extending the handle somewhat (Figure 5.4a). Use a firm, continuous pull toward the lower rib cage while leading the turn with your head to the opposite direction (Figure 5.4b). Use your legs and knees to swivel the board around, and lean your upper body away to keep the leading edge of the board up. Keep the handle close to your back, and regrasp with your free hand in the back position (Figure 5.4c). To come forward again, simply let go with one hand, keep the handle in close, and lean away as you come around to the front (Figure 5.4d).

a

Figure 5.4. Kneeboard turnaround (cont. on next page).

b

c

d

Figure 5.4. Kneeboard turnaround (cont.).

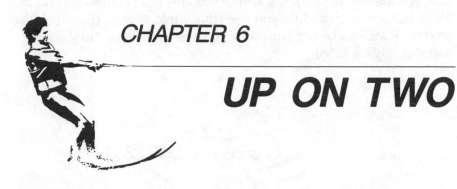

CHAPTER 6

UP ON TWO

Getting up from deep water on a pair of water skis is not very difficult, if you are prepared. Unfortunately, most skiers make their first attempts with only a vague understanding of what they're supposed to do. In this chapter you will learn how to do a deepwater start properly so that you won't have to suffer the grueling trial-and-error process most skiers go through. First you'll learn the right technique for the start, and you'll practice it on land. Then you'll practice putting on and controlling your skis in the water. You'll also learn what mistakes beginners commonly make, so that you can avoid them.

A Dry Run

The correct position for a two-ski deepwater start is similar to that for doing a cannonball into a swimming pool. Your knees should be drawn up to your chest and your shoulders hunched forward against them. The skis are parallel and close together, not quite touching, with the tips showing above the water. Your arms are outstretched on either side of your knees. The handle is held at the ends with the knuckles up, fingernails down (Figure 6.1a).

During the start, you want to freeze in this cannonball position and let the boat pull you up on top of the water like a sled. You should not try to stand up at first. As the boat accelerates and the skis rise to the surface, you merely tilt forward slightly until you are sitting on your heels (Figure 6.1b, c). This squat position, rather than the normal stand-up skiing position, should be your goal on your first attempts. Standing up right away will only invite a fall.

Stay down and ski in the squat position for a slow count of 10, or until you are sure of yourself and your skis are under complete control. Then and only then should you rise slowly into skiing position, with your back and head erect, arms straight, knees well bent, and skis close together (Figure 6.1d).

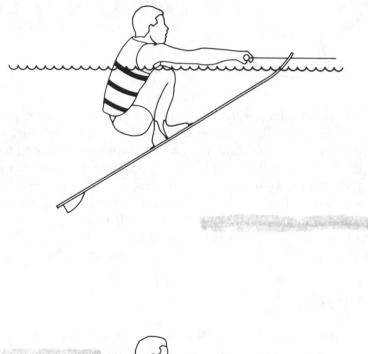

a

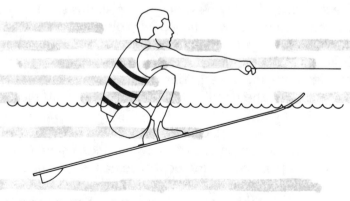

b

Figure 6.1. The two-ski deepwater start (cont. on next page).

c

d

Figure 6.1.   The two-ski deepwater start (cont.).

With a ski rope and the help of another person, practice the start on land as shown in Figure 6.2. Sit down in the cannonball position—chest up against the knees, arms outstretched, feet shoulder-width apart and tucked up close to the buttocks. Hold the handle and have your helper be the "boat." When your helper pulls, simply rock forward onto your haunches without otherwise changing your position. Remain there for a moment and picture yourself skiing that way. Then stand slowly, without leaning back against the pull of the rope.

Sound simple? That's really all there is to it.

Balancing During the Start

A lot of first-time skiers mistakenly believe that they have to struggle to get up. If you stay crouched down in the cannonball position, the start won't take much effort because the boat will do all the work. All you have to do is balance from front-to-back and side-to-side.

a

Figure 6.2. Dry land drill (cont. on next page).

b

c

Figure 6.2. Dry land drill (cont.).

If you go limp as a dish rag when the boat goes, you will get pulled on your face, so you must brace yourself to stay over your binders and not get pulled too far forward. This does *not* mean leaning back or pulling on the rope, because if you do you will over-compensate and fall backwards. Just keep your ankles, legs, back, and shoulders rigid to maintain the cannonball position as the boat pulls.

To keep your balance from side to side, you must hold your skis together and steer by moving the rope from one side to the other as needed. It will take only a slight movement to compensate for any tendency to fall over. If you begin to tilt to one side, shift the handle in that direction a few inches to counteract the lean and maintain your equilibrium. Again, however, it's important that you do not pull on the rope.

Putting On and Controlling the Skis in the Water

It is very important that you learn how to put on and control the skis in the water before attempting to ski. Many skiers are so exasperated after wrestling with the skis in the water that they lose the mental and physical coordination needed for a successful start. It may be much easier to put on your skis while on the dock or in shallow water; but sooner or later you're going to fall far from shore where you can't touch bottom, so you'll be much better off if you learn this basic skill beforehand.

Your binders should be adjusted to a proper fit before getting into the water. Check the fit by putting on your skis on the dock or in the boat. Always wet the binder and your foot thoroughly before putting on a ski. This lubricates the binder and makes it easier to put on. If you adjust the binders when dry, they will feel loose in the water.

To put a ski on, bend the heel piece of the binder over to one side and force your foot into the toe piece as far as it will go (Figure 6.3a). Next, using both hands, grip the top of the heel piece with the thumbs inside and pull up while pushing your heel down flat against the ski (Figure 6.3b, c). This action is much like pulling on a boot. If you have trouble putting the ski on, chances are good that your foot is not far enough into the toe piece before pulling on the heel piece.

The binders should be snug but comfortable. You should be able to lift each ski without feeling as if it's going to come off, but the binders

a

b

c

Figure 6.3.   Putting on a ski binder.

should not pinch or be uncomfortably tight. If either binder is too loose or too tight, take your foot out, adjust the heel piece, and try again. If the binders are still too loose even though they have been adjusted all the way in, try wearing a pair of athletic socks.

When the binders have been adjusted, put on your ski vest and get in the water. Although the technique is similar to that used on land, putting the skis on in the water is trickier because you don't have anything solid to push against. Don't worry, because with a little practice it will seem easy.

With one hand, bend the heel piece over as you did on land, but this time hold it there by grasping the edge of the ski. Grasp the toe piece with your other hand. Sink the ski under you and insert your foot in the toe piece as far as you can. Next, pull up sharply on the heel piece with both hands while plunging your heel down against the ski. If this is done in one quick motion, the water will provide enough resistance to push against, and the foot will slip into place. A long, slow pull will only result in tilting the ski forward. As when pulling on a boot, keep your foot at right angles and push with your leg. Try to keep the ski underneath you and work on top of it. Don't let it float to the surface. Hunch forward with your head and shoulders to keep the ski under water. Take a breath and put your face in the water if necessary.

When you have the first ski on, keep it under you by drawing your leg up close to your chest. Now, put on the other ski in the same manner. With both hands occupied and one ski already on, you may experience a tendency to roll over out of position while doing this. Get well balanced prior to sinking the second ski; work quickly and use the ski that's already on as an underwater stabilizer. The water resistance against it, and against the ski you are putting on, will help you brace momentarily.

It will feel strange at first to have both skis on your feet. You can't kick, and the buoyant skis will try to float you out of position. Keep your body in a compact ball and stay on top of your binders by hunching forward. Tread water with your arms for stability. The tips of the skis should be together near or just above the surface (Figure 6.4).

If you lose control and come apart, don't panic. Recover by floating on your side and drawing your knees up towards your chest, bringing the skis together again slowly (Figure 6.5a). From here you can sink

Figure 6.4. Treading water with skis on.

a

Figure 6.5. Regaining control of skis (cont. on next page).

the skis and use your arms to rotate into an upright position (Figure 6.5b-d). Relax and move slowly. Flow into position rather than trying to fight it.

Practice until you have the knack of putting on the skis and maintaining control of them. When you water-ski you will be faced with having to put on your skis again and again, so spend as long as necessary to be able to handle them in the water with confidence.

b

c

Figure 6.5. Regaining control of skis (cont. on next page).

d

Figure 6.5. Regaining control of skis (cont.).

Hit It!

Now it's time to crank up the boat and go water skiing. You are better prepared at this point than are most people who attempt to ski, so you have half the battle won. You know what to do and you can handle the skis in the water. Consequently, you can turn your full attention to getting up.

Okay, you're in the water with your vest and skis on, and you've told the driver to take up slack. Orient yourself so that you are facing the towboat, and guide the towrope loosely through your fingers as the boat idles out. Look for the handle to come up, and be ready to begin moving as soon as you grab hold of it. Grasp the handle with both hands and quickly maneuver it to equalize the pull so that you are not pulled over.

As the boat drags you slowly through the water, use the tension on the rope to steer. Remember to keep your arms straight and to the outside of your legs, your chest up against your knees, your head up, and your skis together with the tips out of the water and with the towrope between them.

Take your time. Remember that you are in command. You tell the driver when to idle forward and when to put the motor in neutral, so proceed only if you are ready. Don't worry about inconveniencing the driver.

When all the slack has been taken out and you are ready, tell the driver to "Hit it." Hold the handle low as the boat accelerates. Look ahead at the boat and not down at your skis. Hold your cannonball position and let the boat pull you up. Stay crouched down once you are up on top of the water. Then when you feel steady, stand up gradually. Figure 6.6 shows you how the start should look.

a

b

Figure 6.6. Right up the first time (cont. on next page)!

c

d

Figure 6.6. Right up the first time (cont.)!

How did you do? If you followed instructions to the letter, you got right up and experienced the thrill of skiing on water (Figure 6.7). If you made it, congratulations. If you didn't, don't feel alone. Few people are successful on their very first try. Give the "skier OK" sign, recover your skis, and try again.

Figure 6.7. Congratulations, you're a water-skier!

If you fell, try to analyze why. Did you pull on the rope or stand up right away? You may have done several things incorrectly. If you are not sure why you fell, ask someone in the boat to tell you what they think you did wrong. You want to concentrate on not making the same mistake twice, of course, but don't become so absorbed with correcting one mistake that you forget the other important points. If you feel that the boat is accelerating too fast or not fast enough for you, let the driver know. Too much or too little power on takeoff can make getting up more difficult than it needs to be.

Two-Ski Deepwater Start
1. Hold cannonball tuck position throughout start.
2. Don't pull on rope.
3. When skiing in good control, stand up slowly.

Common Pitfalls

Almost all beginners' falls during takeoffs can be traced to one of four basic mistakes. By knowing what they are and striving to avoid them, you can prevent a lot of unnecessary spills.

1. Pulling on the towrope. Many skiers almost instinctively pull on the rope when the boat begins to accelerate. The result is almost always a backward fall. If you pull on the rope and then stop pulling, the boat will probably yank your arms out straight again, and you'll fall "over the handlebars." Fight the instinct to pull on the rope. Be prepared for it. Steer with the rope from side to side but don't haul in on it.

2. Standing up too soon. It is also a natural reaction to begin standing as soon as the boat goes. The trouble is that by standing you are no longer a compact ball. You become top-heavy and tend to fall over. Your skis will also have a much greater tendency to spread apart. Stay down on your heels until well after you are up and skiing in good control. Don't be in a hurry to stand up. You can ski half-way around the lake in the squat position, if necessary.

3. Not keeping the body centered over the skis. Staying centered over your skis is a matter of balance and feel. Backward falls are usually caused by pulling on the rope and forward falls are from going limp. Falls to the side generally indicate a problem with steering—failing to keep the skis pointed straight ahead or to use the tension on the rope to help maintain balance.

4. Not keeping the skis close together. Having the skis split apart on takeoff is usually caused by standing up too soon. If you stay in a cannonball tuck during the start, your skis will stay together. Keep the skis parallel and just slightly apart.

Teaching Others How to Water-Ski

The scene that follows, or something similar to it, is one that is repeated countless times each summer on lakes and rivers throughout the United States.

A group of friends has gone to the lake for a day of boating and water skiing. With them is a 12-year-old girl who wants to learn to ski. The owner of the boat, considered by the group to be the expert, assumes the role of instructor and in less than two minutes he has given her a crash course in how to water ski. Then he straps a ski vest on her that is much too large. A little bewildered, she is hoisted overboard and the skis are tossed to her.

Struggling for the better part of 10 minutes, she finally manages to get both skis on but discovers that one is too loose. She takes it off but is unable to adjust the binder. The boat circles and picks up the ski. The binder is made smaller and the ski is handed back to the girl who, after several tries, has it on again. Soon, however, both skis have floated behind her, tips crossed, and she is hopelessly contorted. Thrashing about in the oversized vest, she eventually regains her position. The boat idles out; she reaches for the handle and yells "Hit it!" The boat takes off, she gets part way up, totters a bit and in an effort to recover her balance, she pulls on the handle. She topples over backwards with a splash. One ski comes off.

Several more tries are made. Each time, for one reason or another, she falls, and each time one or both skis come off and have to be put back on again. With each spill people in the boat and on shore shout words of advice that only serve to make her increasingly confused and angry. She wants very much to get up, but she becomes more and more discouraged. Water gets up her nose each time she falls. Finally, exhausted and cold, she calls it quits and huddles on the beach with a towel around her shoulders as the others take their turns. Mr. Ski Instructor tells her not to worry, they'll try it again after a while. She's not so sure she wants to go through that again, whether later that day or ever.

Such ineffectual or even harmful instruction is unfortunately the norm because, although they are well-meaning, the vast majority of water-skiers who attempt to teach others have little idea how to go about it. As a result, the beginners who learn to ski often do so in spite of their instructors rather than because of them. Here is some advice and a couple of proven techniques that you can use to increase your effectiveness when teaching others how to do a two-ski deepwater start.

Applied Psychology

Teaching someone how to get up on water skis is largely a matter of putting yourself in their binders, so to speak, particularly if you are working with a youngster. Because you already know how to ski, what may seem perfectly obvious to you may not be obvious to someone who has never been on skis before. You must force yourself to see things from the learner's perspective.

Beginners may be frightened of the water or apprehensive of being pulled far from shore. They may fear being injured. They may be afraid of the powerful motor. They may be embarrassed in front of those who are watching. Be aware of these and other fears that may enter into the situation. Be understanding and do what you can to make the beginner feel at ease. Take each step slowly, and do not move on to the next stage until the learner is ready. Lavish praise when progress is made; be patient when it is not.

Something else to remember when dealing with kids is that small bodies can get cold quickly in water. Even a few minutes in water that seems quite comfortable to an adult can sap the strength and coordination of a child who is not swimming vigorously. Don't force a child to continue if he or she appears chilled.

Kids often get up right away if they understand what they're supposed to do and are given some assistance in the awkward business of getting the skis on and holding the starting position. Keep instructions simple and few. Kids can be easily confused if overloaded with information. Whenever possible, demonstrate rather than give verbal instructions. Limit the number of attempts made in any one session.

Help in the Water

Putting on and controlling the skis in the water is often the most difficult task for beginners to master, so the time taken to learn how is well spent. Have students practice for several sessions, if necessary, before attempting any starts. The better they are at handling the skis in the water, the quicker they will learn how to ski.

If a learner has particular difficulty putting on skis or controlling them once they are on, it may be best to get in the water to help. You can also help the learner maintain the starting position by holding him or her by the waist from behind or by reaching around and grasping the shins or ankles and holding the learner in the cannonball tuck (Figure 6.8). This can be done in deeper water, if you wear a ski vest.

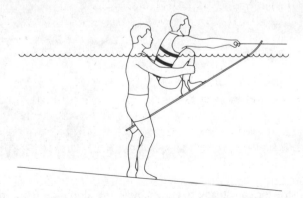

Figure 6.8. Helping beginner hold the starting position in the water.

The main disadvantage of this method is that the skier may fall after having gone quite a few yards and you will be left a good distance behind.

Skiing Alongside

Learning to water-ski is much like learning to ride a bicycle: Once you have the feel of pedaling and balancing at the same time, you've got it made. But someone must support the bike until you get the hang of it, or else it must be equipped with training wheels. By skiing alongside your learner, it is possible for you to be the "training wheels."

Assuming that your boat has adequate power to pull two skiers easily, you can ski beside the beginner using a rope the same length and steady him or her when getting up. If it is a small child, this can be done by grasping the top of his or her vest during the start. Otherwise you can hold the beginner's near arm as in Figure 6.9, or, for additional support, you can reach across and hold the opposite arm above the elbow.

By skiing alongside, you can prevent your skier from standing too soon or from pulling on the towrope. You can also talk to the learner during the start, something that's nearly impossible when you are in the boat or on shore. If the skier falls, let go of your own towrope immediately. It's not only more reassuring for the beginner to have someone alongside in the water after a fall, but you can also help recover and put on the skis. The driver can then idle back as you discuss with the skier what caused the fall.

a

Figure 6.9. Instructor can steady beginner by skiing alongside (cont. on next page).

b

c

Figure 6.9.   Instructor can steady beginner by skiing alongside (cont.).

Trainers

Special trainer skis are available that can be used effectively to teach small children. The trainers consist of a set of small skis that are tied together. The towrope is attached to the front crosstie, so that the child merely stands in place and the whole apparatus is towed like a sled. Trainers have even been used to teach toddlers how to ski without the use of a boat; the adult simply pulls the child by hand along a beach (Figure 6.10). The decision as to when a child is ready to learn how to ski is, of course, an individual one that has to be carefully considered by the parents.

Figure 6.10. Trainers can be used to teach very young children. Photo courtesy of Casad Manufacturing Corp. Printed with permission.

CHAPTER 7

TWO-SKI CONFIDENCE

You most likely will feel pretty unstable when you first get up on skis. Like the first time you ride a bike or use ice skates, you will be wobbly until you get your "sea legs." This chapter will help you get over the awkward stage quickly and help you learn the skills needed to maneuver on two skis. It will take some time and practice, but before long you will develop a confidence in your ability that will make your skiing safer and more fun.

Two-Ski Posture

Are you bent forward at the waist when you ski, as in Figure 7.1? This position is quite normal for a beginner, but it is very tiring and does not

Figure 7.1. Skiing like this is awkward and tiring.

permit proper control of the skis. To improve your stability, straighten your back and shoulders until they are upright. At the same time, lower your hips and bend your knees as if you were starting to do a deep knee bend. Keep your head up, bring your skis close together, and lower the handle slightly. Figure 7.2 shows the correct two-ski posture. This position—with the head up, back erect, and knees bent—is fundamental to all water skiing, so concentrate on it as you are learning.

Figure 7.2.   Ski with back upright and knees bent for good control.

Good Water Skiing Posture
1. Head and back erect.
2. Knees well bent.
3. Skis together (on two skis).
4. Lower the handle slightly

Changing Directions

Once you feel stable riding straight ahead, try weaving back and forth between the wakes. To turn a bicycle you point the front wheel the way you want to go and simultaneously lean in that direction. Similarly, to change direction on water skis you rotate the skis so that they are aimed the way you wish to go, and you lean away from the boat in that direction, causing the skis to tilt or "edge" at an angle. The more the skis are turned and the harder you lean, the faster you will cut or move to one side. Bend your knees and pull in and down slightly on the handle. Practice weaving back and forth within the wake and get used to the skis. Keep the skis close together and parallel when turning.

Crossing the Wake

Now that you have the feel of the skis and can control your direction, the next step is to cross the boat wake. Like all waves, the wake is a hill of water that moves along the surface. Skiing behind the boat, you are moving at the same speed as the wake, so that it appears to be stationary.

To cross the wake you must climb this hill of water. If you try to cross it slowly with your skis parallel to it and without much tilt or "edge," you will slide back down in the middle. To get across you must get a running start (Figure 7.3a), keep your skis on edge all the way up and over to maintain your momentum, and cross the crest at an angle (Figure 7.3b, c). Do not let up on your pull or your lean until both skis have crossed the crest (the peak of the wake). Keep your skis close together, or you may get hung up on the crest.

Depending on the type of boat you are using and your speed, the wake may be particularly large or turbulent. There may even be a double crest. If any of these conditions make it difficult to cross the wake, try a slightly higher boat speed. Also, experiment with different tilt settings on outboards and take any extra weight out of the boat. Make certain that the weight in the boat is balanced from side to side, because too much weight on one side can make the wake on that side much larger.

Outside the wake you experience the true freedom of water skiing. You can swing out as wide as you wish by cutting—leaning and pulling—harder. When you stop cutting, the pull on the rope causes you to drift back in toward the wake. Because of this, it is easier to cross the wake from the outside heading in, but you must remember to cross the crest at an angle and with your skis together. If you encounter rough water or other boat wakes while skiing outside the wake, flex your knees more to cushion the ride.

a

b

Figure 7.3. Crossing the wake (cont. on next page).

c

Figure 7.3. Crossing the wake (cont.).

Crossing the Wake
1. Cut continuously up and over wake.
2. Cross crest at an angle.

Jumping the Wake

When you can cross both wakes with confidence, you may want to get a little fancier and jump the wake. It is easier to get the skis into the air by cutting from the outside of the wake in because of the angle of pull and because the wake is normally steeper. Choose a boat speed that will give you a good size wake and enough speed to cut. Ski outside the wake 10 to 15 feet, then rotate and point your ski tips toward the center of the wakes. Edge your skis and cut all the way to the wake (Figure 7.4a). With your skis close together, spring up by snapping your legs straight and straightening your back. Begin your spring at the base of the wake so that it is completed by the time you reach the crest. If you wait too late, your spring will be completed in the air and will do no good. Your cut and your spring off the wake will send you flying (Figure 7.4b). Keep your head up, eyes focused ahead, and your skis together with the tips up. Compensate for the impact of landing by flexing your knees like shock absorbers and by pulling in on the towrope by tucking your elbows into your hips (Figure 7.4c).

Jumping the Wake
1. Cut briskly from outside of wake in.
2. Spring up, legs straight at crest.
3. Skis together in air, tips up.
4. Absorb landing with knees.

a

Figure 7.4. Jumping the wake (cont. on next page).

b

c

Figure 7.4. Jumping the wake (cont.).

Turns

One thing that you will learn quickly on water skis is the effect of centrifugal force. If the boat turns to the left and you cut out to the right at the same time, you are going to get whipped out fast. Depending on your initial speed, how tight the boat is turning, and how hard you are cutting, your speed can be increased significantly, perhaps even so much that you lose control. Conversely, if you cut out to the same side that the boat is turning, you will lose speed and bog down in the water. This is why it is important that you have good communication with your driver so that each of you will be able to anticipate the actions of the other. On your first couple of rides, stay within the wakes when the boat is turning.

If you do get whipped out, or for any other reason find that you are going too fast outside the wakes and are in danger of losing control, you can slow down by using the "snow plow" technique. First, stop leaning to prevent any further increase in speed. Once you have both skis riding flat, apply pressure to the inside edges of your skis by skiing knock-kneed while spreading the skis apart to form a wedge, as shown in Figure 7.5. You can practice this by letting go of the rope and snow-plowing to a stop.

Figure 7.5. Use the snow plow to slow down.

Rope Handling

It is best to keep your arms almost straight when learning how to get up. Later on, as you get better, you will discover that you will have better control if you bend your arms more. Hold the handle about waist level with your arms moderately flexed to act as shock absorbers and ready to pull in or extend the handle slightly with changes in tension on the rope. When cutting out it's most effective to pull the handle in toward the belt line by tucking your elbows in toward your hips (Figure 7.6). When decelerating in relation to the boat, as when you are preparing to turn back toward the wake from the outside, extend the handle slowly and smoothly in the direction of the pull, to prevent too much slack (Figure 7.7). Never raise the handle above your head to compensate for slack; instead, extend the handle until the speed has been equalized, then pull it in toward your waist.

Watch an experienced slalom skier run the slalom course, for an exaggerated illustration of these principles. As the skier approaches a buoy the handle is extended smoothly. As the turn is completed the skier leans back and pulls the handle toward the waist to accelerate. There is no slack in the rope even though the turn has been sharp.

Learn to use your arms to work the rope effectively. They are the vital links that transmit the power of the boat to your skis.

Figure 7.6. Pull handle toward waist when cutting out.

Figure 7.7.   Slowly extend the handle toward the boat to control slack.

Landings

When you have skied long enough and are ready to stop, the easiest way to end your ride (after making sure the observer is paying attention), is to simply let go of the handle and have the boat come back and pick you up. Often, however, you will want to start from and return to shore.

For safe shore landings, the towboat should parallel the shoreline at a constant speed and you should swing out and drop off slowly. Never attempt to land close to or sit on a dock or pier or ski up on land. It is very easy to misjudge your speed and the consequences of a collision are just too great to risk. Land a reasonable distance out and then swim in.

If you make a mistake and come in too fast, snowplow to slow down. If you are still in danger of a collision, sit down on the back of your skis and dig your hands in the water (Figure 7.8) or, as a last resort, deliberately fall over to one side.

Never make a shore landing where other boats, skiers, and swimmers are congregated. Not only is there a danger that you may hit someone, but also you cannot be certain that other boats that may be taking off will see you or your towboat. Land only into uncrowded shore areas.

Figure 7.8.   Stopping in an emergency.

The Dock Start

A sitting dock start involves a more sudden pull than a deepwater start, but it should give you no trouble at this stage of your development. Ideally, the dock should be just high enough that your ankles are at water level when you are sitting on the edge. The dock surface where you sit should be free of splinters. Also, there should be no cleats, nails, posts, hooks, or other protrusions nearby that could snag your towrope or swimsuit.

With your skis on, sit on the edge of the dock and then coil the towrope neatly and place the coils in the water in front of you. (For safety, do not pay out the rope by hand.) Tell the driver to idle forward. Just before the last coil of rope is pulled tight, tell the driver to "Hit it." As the rope snaps tight, shift your weight from the dock to the skis. Crouch down and hold the handle in close so that you don't get pulled too far forward. Figure 7.9 shows the dock start sequence.

If you give the boat too much rope, it will be going too fast when the rope tightens, and either you will get pulled over your ski tips or the handle will pop out of your hands. If you allow too little rope to

a

b

Figure 7.9. Sitting dock start (cont. on next page).

c

Figure 7.9. Sitting dock start (cont.).

pay out before telling the driver to go, you may not have sufficient speed and you may sink as soon as you leave the dock. It may take several tries to get the timing right.

Sitting Dock Start
1. Timing is most important.
2. Crouch down and pull in as rope tightens.

Skiing Double

It's fun to ski double with a friend or another family member, but you must coordinate your movements to assure a safe and pleasant ride. Obviously, you want to avoid colliding with each other. At the start you must stay separated so that you do not interfere with your partner's takeoff, and once you are up you cannot cut back and forth as freely as when you are skiing by yourself (Figure 7.10). You must also cooperate when turning. If you force the other skier to the inside of a turn, he or she will lose speed and may fall. When you are on the outside of a turn, pull out slightly to give your partner room to maintain his or her own speed.

You should not attempt to cross under the other skier's rope. Make sure also that your towropes are of equal length. If either of you falls, the other should let go immediately. Stay together. Otherwise the driver will be obligated to maintain skiing speed on the way back to the fallen skier, which is unsafe. Furthermore, it is dangerous to attempt to ski over or to pick up the towrope of another skier who has fallen. Instead, let go of your own rope and stay with your partner.

Figure 7.10. Cooperation is needed when skiing double.

CHAPTER 8

GRADUATION TO ONE SKI

As soon as you start to feel at home on two skis, you will probably be thinking ahead about skiing on a single ski. Once you discover the fun of carving graceful turns on a slalom and sending up curtains of spray, you may never want to return to two skis again.

The easiest way to learn to ski on a single ski is to start out on two skis and then drop one. Being right- or left-handed has little bearing on which leg you will favor, so how do you know which ski to drop? You can find out quickly and easily by standing on a solid surface with your knees flexed and then simply lifting one foot a few inches off the ground. The leg you balance on is by nature the one you want to ski on. The leg you raise is your "drop ski" side.

The Skier's Salute

Before dropping one ski, practice lifting the ski clear of the water for as long as you can. This maneuver is known as the "skier's salute" (Figure 8.1). A pair of combination skis is ideal for learning the skier's salute and also for learning how to ski on one ski. Your boat speed should be fast enough that you don't bog down when you shift all of your weight to one ski, but not so fast that you are not in control. Get in a good skiing position with your knees well bent, your head up, and your back erect. Hold the handle about waist level and shift it to one side, directly in line with your "skiing" ski. Now, lift the other ski directly off the water a few inches. Be sure to keep the tip of the

Figure 8.1. The skier's salute.

ski up so that it doesn't dig in and trip you. Look ahead at the boat, not down at the water.

Try holding the ski off the water a little longer each time. You don't have to hold it very high, just enough so that it is off the water. Practice for several sessions until you can hold the ski up easily for a slow count of five or more. When you are stable doing the skier's salute, it's time to drop one.

Dropping One Ski

Make sure that the binder of your drop ski is adjusted so that it is very loose and will come off easily when you want it to. This time, instead of lifting the ski, slide it back 6 to 12 inches and lift the heel of your foot off the ski while keeping part of your weight on the ball of your foot still in the binder (Figure 8.2a). Balance like this until you are ready to drop the ski. Keep your skiing knee very bent and your arms in. Hold the handle in line with your "skiing" ski and with the knuckles of both hands on top.

Now the moment of truth has come. When you are in good balance, let the drop ski slide off behind you by extending your leg to the rear and pointing your toes (Figure 8.2b). Do not kick the ski off because the sudden movement may upset your balance.

a

b

Figure 8.2. Dropping one ski (cont. on next page).

What you do next will depend on how you feel you will balance best. You can keep the free foot lifted, as if doing the skier's salute, or you can drag it in the water lightly, with the toes pointed backward, to act as an outrigger (Figure 8.2c). Whichever you do, do not be in a rush to put your free foot on the ski. Ski like a crane on one leg for a while, with your "skiing" knee bent, until you are in full control. Then carefully place your free foot lightly on the back of the ski as close to your front foot as possible. If you can easily find the rear binder, go ahead and put your foot in it. However, the most important thing for now is to get your foot on the ski so that you can rest your skiing leg. Don't look down or spend time feeling around for the binder with your foot. Just get your foot on the ski close behind the front binder. Step on top of the rear binder if necessary.

Put weight on the rear foot very slowly and carefully, making sure that the foot is centered from side to side. If the ski begins to wobble, move your foot farther forward on the ski. With your rear foot on the ski at last, you can rest your front leg. When your front leg is fully rested, you can reposition the rear foot, if necessary, or put it in the rear binder if you didn't at first. Make sure your foot is fully inserted in the rear binder or the ski will not track straight.

c

Figure 8.2. Dropping one ski (cont.).

The observer should keep an eye on the location of the dropped ski, and the driver should return and pick it up at the first opportunity. It will certainly be damaged or destroyed if it is run over by another boat. Whenever you plan to drop a ski, choose an area where no other boats are operating.

Dropping One Ski

1. Slide drop ski back, lift heel out of binder. *Lean Back Somewhat More*
2. Bend knees.
3. Let drop ski slide off behind.
4. Balance on one leg before slowly putting free foot on ski.

Skiing on One

Your body position on one ski should be the same as on two skis, except that with one foot on the back of the ski you will be leaning back somewhat more (Figure 8.3). Keep your torso upright and your head up,

Figure 8.3.   On a single ski, ride with back upright and both knees bent.

and flex your arms for good rope control. Lean back comfortably against the pull of the rope with your weight evenly distributed on both legs. Bend both knees to act as shock absorbers. If the heel of your rear foot rises off the ski, you are favoring your front leg too much. If you can't keep both feet flat on the ski, either your rear foot is not all the way in the binder or the ski is too big for you.

Changing directions on one ski is accomplished the same way as on two—your body lean causes the ski to tilt on edge and scoot to the side. Without a second ski to act as an outrigger, your balance is more dependent on maintaining equilibrium between your lean and the pull of the rope. This is why it is very important that you keep your arms and knees flexed at all times.

Wake crossing on one ski is easy if you cut across the crest of the wake at an angle, with your arms and knees bent. Cutting outside the wake on a slalom is one of the great joys of water skiing. With some practice you will be able to lean hard and see rainbows in your spray and hear your ski hum as it knifes through the water. Pull with the handle near your inside hip (left hip if you are cutting to the right) and with your shoulders back. Push with your legs but keep your knees flexed (Figure 8.4).

Figure 8.4. Cutting outside the wake on one ski.

Deepwater Start

The one-ski deepwater start is somewhat more difficult than the two-ski start because with only one ski you have half the planing area and there is also a greater tendency to twist out of position on takeoff. Use a wide ski to make the start as easy as possible.

Your body position should be similar to that for the two-ski start: your skiing leg bent, your chest pressed forward against the knee, and your arms out straight. Your free leg should be trailed out behind you (Figure 8.5a).

As when making a two-ski start, you should not stand immediately. If you do, you may push the tip of the ski under water. Stay low until the ski begins to plane (Figure 8.5b). Be patient and let the boat do the work. Use your free leg as a stabilizer; as you accelerate, the water pressure against the leg will actually provide some additional planing surface that will help you get up. When you have gained sufficient speed, rise up slowly and draw your free leg in (Figure 8.5c). When you are fully planed off, you can kick into the rear binder.

If you are not successful getting up this way, try it with both feet on the ski. Although most people will find it even harder to balance this way, some, especially lighter individuals, may find it an easier way to get up. Be sure, however, to keep the ski angled as flat as possible by pulling it up close to your body. If you lean back on your rear foot and stand the ski up straight, it will drag through the water and make your start more difficult.

a

Figure 8.5. One-ski deepwater start (cont. on next page).

b

c

Figure 8.5. One-ski deepwater start (cont.).

One Ski Deepwater Start
1. Ski leg bent up to chest, free leg trailing behind.
2. Stay crouched down until ski is planing.
3. Use free leg as stabilizer.

Standing Dock Start

The standing dock start is a fun and easy way to take off on a single ski, but try it only after you have gained some experience skiing on your slalom.

With your ski on, stand with your weight on your free foot at the edge of the dock, with the front of the ski extending over the water (Figure 8.6a). Coil the rope, place the coils in the water, and tell the

a

Figure 8.6. Standing dock start (cont. on next page).

driver to take up slack. When all of the loops have been pulled out, but before the rope has been pulled tight, yell "Hit it." As the rope tightens, step off the dock and place the ski on the water, making sure that it is pointed straight ahead (Figure 8.6b). Pull the handle in and resist the pull as you settle in the water. Use your free foot as a stabilizer. If timed correctly, the step off the dock will move you at the same speed as the accelerating boat and you will ski away with ease (Figure 8.6c). Step off too soon and the ski will sink. Step off too late and the sudden pull may yank you on your face. Pretty soon you will be able to time the start perfectly.

Standing Dock Start
1. Stand near edge of dock, ski extending over water.
2. Timing is most important.
3. Place ski on water and step off when rope snaps tight.
4. Pull handle in, use free leg as stabilizer.

b

Figure 8.6. Standing dock start (cont. on next page).

c

Figure 8.6. Standing dock start (cont.).

Teaching Others How to Ski on One Ski

When teaching someone how to ride a single ski, you can help the learner balance on one leg by skiing alongside and holding the learner's arm or shoulder, as in Figure 8.7, as long as is necessary for the learner to make the transition to one ski. If either of you should fall, the other should drop into the water immediately so that the boat does not have to maintain skiing speed on its return.

Figure 8.7. Instructor steadying skier on one ski.

CHAPTER 9

DEVELOPING SLALOM TECHNIQUE

Up to this point you have learned how to cut out to either side of the wake on your slalom ski and throw a lot of spray, but you're really not slaloming yet because when you straighten up and stop pulling, you drift back toward the wake. To do continuous slalom turns back and forth as if running the slalom course, you must learn to cut *toward* the wake to give yourself enough momentum to carry you far out to the opposite side. Cutting toward the wake will seem strange at first, but once you get used to it you will discover that it is the key to the exhilaration of slalom skiing.

Begin by weaving back and forth between the wakes. As you snake from one side of the wake to the other, notice how your body and ski work together. When you move to the right, you point the ski in that direction and lean so that the ski tilts onto its right edge. To change directions, you stop pulling, straighten up, swing the ski around so that it is pointed to the left, and then lean to the left. As you shift your weight, the ski "changes edges"; that is, the ski first flattens out, then tilts on its other edge. Full slalom turns are magnified versions of these elementary turns. The lean and the edge change are simply more pronounced.

The Slalom Turn

As shown in Figure 9.1, a complete slalom turn has three phases: pre-turn, turn, and acceleration. The acceleration phase (the pull toward the wake) has already been mentioned. However, you cannot make a controlled turn if you are going too fast. You must slow down after crossing the wakes. This is the function of the preturn. In this phase you stop pulling and begin a gradual turn while slowly extending the handle toward the boat. This causes the ski to ride deeper on its inside edge, slowing you down. The turn is completed when the ski comes fully around and you pull the handle in toward your waist and lean away to accelerate toward the wake. The art of slaloming lies in accelerating and decelerating smoothly between controlled turns.

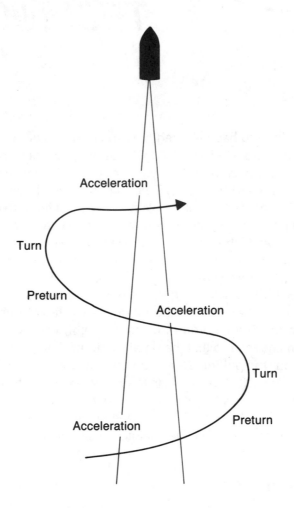

Figure 9.1.   The three phases of a slalom turn.

Your first slalom turns outside the wake should be done slowly and gradually, not far outside the wake and with very little pull or lean. Your objective is to make smooth, even turns without slack rope. Once you have mastered the technique of carving a smooth turn, you can work up to making tighter turns farther out.

Start by skiing 15 to 20 feet outside the right wake. Stop leaning away from the boat, then make a broad, sweeping turn to the left, as if you were skiing around something in the water. As you straighten up and the ski begins to flatten out, slowly extend the handle a little toward the boat. Pull the handle back in toward your waist again as the turn is completed and you cut to the left. If you stab the handle out quickly, you will create slack. Let it out slowly and smoothly, just enough to maintain an even tension on the rope throughout the turn. Never raise the handle above your head in an effort to take up slack. (As you get better and make sharper turns, you will let go with the outside hand and extend the handle even more with the inside arm. For now, keep both hands on the handle.)

Before the turn, your ski was pointed away from the wake and the spray was coming off the left edge of your ski. After the turn, your ski is pointed toward the wake and the spray is coming off the right edge. Lean to the left and accelerate back toward the wake. The more you lean and the harder you pull, the faster you will go. For now, don't make a radical cut. Remember, your objective is to make slow, smooth turns.

Don't let up once you reach the wake but keep cutting right through both wakes. After you pass the second wake, stop cutting and begin to straighten up. Let your momentum carry you out to the left side of the wake. As you coast, start making a wide, easy turn back to the right and begin slowly extending the handle toward the boat. This is the preturn. As soon as you begin to lean into the turn (toward the boat) and extend the handle, your ski starts to track on its inside edge and starts to slow you down. Complete the turn 15 to 20 feet outside by bringing the ski completely around, pulling the rope in toward your waist, and leaning harder to your right. Accelerate across both wakes then let up on your pull and begin making a slow turn and handle extension to your left. Once again you will slow down so that you can make a controlled turn. You have now made a complete cycle. As long as you can cut toward the wake and make smooth preturns and controlled turns, you can cut back and forth perpetually like the pendulum of a clock. Figure 9.2 illustrates an elementary slalom turn.

a

b

Figure 9.2. Elementary slalom turn (cont. on next page).

c

d

Figure 9.2.   Elementary slalom turn (cont.).

Strive to make even, symmetrical turns. As you get better you will lean harder, coast out farther on each side, and make sharper turns with your elbow almost touching the water. Because you will be leaning more, the transition during the preturn will become more critical. Don't overextend yourself now. Cut only as hard as your ability to make a smooth turn will allow. Making ragged, jerky turns will only teach you bad habits.

Slalom Turns

1. Pull with shoulders back, back arched, knees flexed.
2. Continue pull across both wakes.
3. Shift weight and extend handle smoothly during preturn.

Preparing for the Course

Attempting the slalom course for the first time can be one of the most humbling experiences for a water-skier. Cutting sharply back and forth on open water is one thing, but turning at six evenly spaced buoys is quite another. The buoys seem to zip by so fast that running the course, at any speed, may seem impossible. Quite often skiers who think they are ready for the course find that they have to get better on open water before challenging the buoys. You, too, should spend a lot of time free-skiing and perfecting your technique by turning at imaginary buoys before trying to run the course.

The key to good slalom technique is not a sharp turn but rather a good, strong pull across both wakes. The power in a slalom pull comes from the back and shoulders, not the arms. Pull with your back arched and your shoulders back, while holding the handle at your hip (Figure 9.3). Push evenly with both legs, but don't lock them straight; keep your knees flexed. Stay back on the ski with your head, hips, and feet in a straight line. Don't allow yourself to get pulled forward or to bend at the waist. For the strongest grip, hold the handle like a baseball bat with the palms facing opposite directions. This is called the opposed grip.

To be effective, the pull must continue across both wakes. This is hard for most beginners to do. It is natural to want to let up and flatten

Figure 9.3. Pull with shoulders back and feet, hips, and head in line.

out the ski at the first wake, but this slows you down too soon and makes your ski bounce excessively. If you approach the wakes back on your ski and in good control, keep leaning and pulling right through them. You may be surprised at how you shoot across the wakes with a minimum of bounce. (Note: If the wakes are monstrous, you will have trouble edging through them properly. Try a faster boat speed and/or a different tilt setting on your motor for a smaller wake.) Don't look down when crossing the wakes but keep your eyes focused on the other side. Practice pulling until you can aggressively slingshot across the wakes in both directions without letting up.

Stop pulling as soon as you cross the second wake. Immediately initiate your preturn and start to extend the handle toward the boat. As you lean harder and cross the wake faster, it will become necessary to extend the handle more by letting go with the outside hand and reaching with the inside arm. Extend the handle slowly and smoothly or you will push slack into the rope. Do not bend forward at the waist in an effort to extend the handle; stay back on your ski with your back straight, head up, and knees bent.

As you lean into the turn and reach with the handle, your ski will begin to track on its inside edge and slow you down. If you continue to pull past the second wake, or if you ride the ski flat without changing edges, you will be going too fast to complete a smooth, sharp turn. When you have made as wide an arc away from the boat as your momentum permits, complete the turn, pull the handle in to the outside hip, lean back with your shoulders, and push with your legs. Figure 9.4 illustrates an advanced slalom turn.

Practice making slalom turns on open water until you can make aggressive cuts and controlled, symmetrical turns as wide of the boat as possible. Concentrate on smooth turns, hard pulls through the wakes, and good body position. When you do it right you will be able to feel the rhythm.

a

Figure 9.4.   Advanced slalom turn (cont. on next page).

b

c

Figure 9.4. Advanced slalom turn (cont. on next page).

d

e

Figure 9.4. Advanced slalom turn (cont.).

Running the Slalom Course

The official slalom course consists of a corridor of buoys through which the boat passes, and six skier-turn buoys placed alternately on either side of the boat path (Figure 9.5). To run the course, the skier must pass through the entrance gate (which is also the first set of boat guides), ski around all six turn buoys in zigzag fashion, and ski out through the exit gate. The skier buoys and gates are red or orange, and the interior boat guide buoys are yellow. Most water ski clubs maintain slalom courses for the use of their members, and many individual slalom skiers install them for their own practice use. Check state and local laws regarding required permits before putting in a slalom course yourself.

When running the slalom course, you have to keep pace with the boat as it charges relentlessly down the center. Since you have to slow down in order to turn at the buoys, you must be able to accelerate and decelerate very quickly. Acceleration, of course, comes from a good, strong pull across both wakes, but you can't pull properly without a controlled set-up and turn. You are already able to make a controlled turn on open water; now you must learn the right way to turn at a buoy.

Beginning slalom skiers almost universally make the mistake of aiming right for the buoy and then attempting a radical hook turn like the dashed line in Figure 9.6. This doesn't work. By heading directly at the buoy, you cross the wakes at a shallow angle that makes your approach to the buoy too narrow, too fast, and too flat (ski not on edge) to make a good turn. Your momentum will tend to carry you far past the buoy, and any attempted hook turn will be ragged and unsteady. Without a good pull you will be late (farther down course) crossing the wake, maybe too late to reach the next buoy.

Like the driver of a race car approaching a hairpin curve, you have to prepare for the turn at the buoy by slowing down and getting wide. To get wide you must cross the wake at a steep angle and aim wide of the buoy, as shown by the solid line in Figure 9.6. Such a broad, looping track will give you the time needed to make your preturn, slow down, and make a controlled turn that will put you in good position for a hard pull back across the wake.

When first learning to run the slalom course, ignore the entrance and exit gates. Get used to making it around all six turn buoys consistently before learning how to negotiate the gates. Choose a boat speed that is

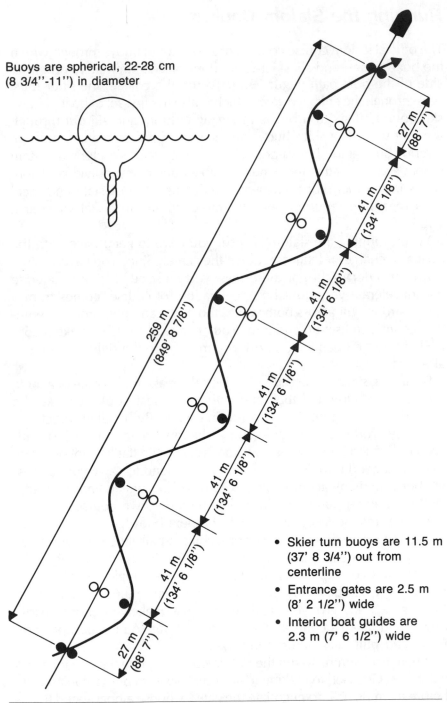

Buoys are spherical, 22-28 cm
(8 3/4''-11'') in diameter

- Skier turn buoys are 11.5 m
  (37' 8 3/4'') out from
  centerline
- Entrance gates are 2.5 m
  (8' 2 1/2'') wide
- Interior boat guides are
  2.3 m (7' 6 1/2'') wide

Figure 9.5.　Diagram of a regulation slalom course.

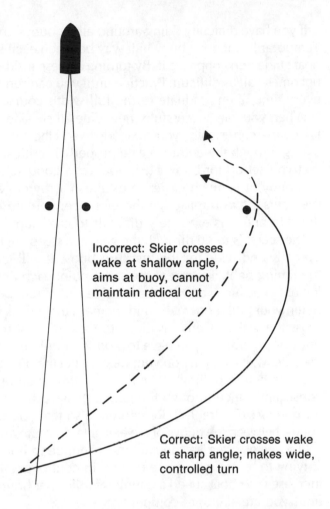

Incorrect: Skier crosses
wake at shallow angle,
aims at buoy, cannot
maintain radical cut

Correct: Skier crosses wake
at sharp angle; makes wide,
controlled turn

Figure 9.6. Turning at a buoy.

relatively slow, yet fast enough that the wake is not too big and you
can accelerate quickly when you pull (between 22 and 28 miles per
hour, depending on your weight). Make a broad turn around the first
buoy, get set for the pull, and cut just on the down-course side of the
buoy. Lean and pull across both wakes for a good angle. Aim wide
of buoy #2 as you begin your reach and preturn. You should arrive
in plenty of time to make a smooth, even turn. By making controlled
turns and strong pulls across the wakes, you "stay ahead" of the course.
If you aim at the buoys, let up on your pulls, or break forward at the
waist, you will "get behind" and eventually will miss a buoy or fall.

If you have difficulty skiing around all six buoys, try a narrow course. Temporarily anchor a buoy half way between each skier buoy and the boat guide buoy opposite it. By turning at these inside buoys, the course becomes half as difficult. Practice until you can run the narrow course every time, then graduate to the full width course.

When you can successfully negotiate all six skier turn buoys of the full course consistently, you are ready to add the entrance and exit gates. Skiing through the entrance gate properly is critical because it is here that you set up for buoy #1. If you get a good setup and turn at the first buoy, it is much easier to establish a rhythm and stay ahead of the course. If you misjudge the entrance, you are behind right from the start and it is extremely difficult to catch up.

The secret is to ski through the gate at a steep angle that will set you up early and wide for the first turn buoy. It will take practice to get the timing right. To start at the same point each time, pull out to the left until you are even with the left-side row of turn buoys in the course. Begin your pull moderately and increase the pull as you approach and cross the wakes. Come as close to the inside of the right-hand gate buoy as possible. If you have to stop your pull in order to get through the gate, wait a bit later on your next try (let the boat get farther through the gate before pulling). Practice your timing and pull until you can consistently slice through the gate at a steep angle in good position for buoy #1 (Figure 9.7). Remember also that you must go out of the course between the buoys of the exit gate on your way out of the course.

Practice as often as you can and continue to hone your technique, striving to be smooth, graceful, and in control at all times. Gradually increase your boat speed a couple of miles per hour as you get better, until you are skiing at competition speeds.

Running The Slalom Course
1. Time cut through gate to set up early for first turn buoy.
2. Make hard pulls that continue across both wakes.
3. Make smooth preturns, aiming wide of turn buoys.

Slalom Competition

The concept of slalom competition is simple. Starting at a minimum speed specified in the rules for his or her division, the skier makes pass

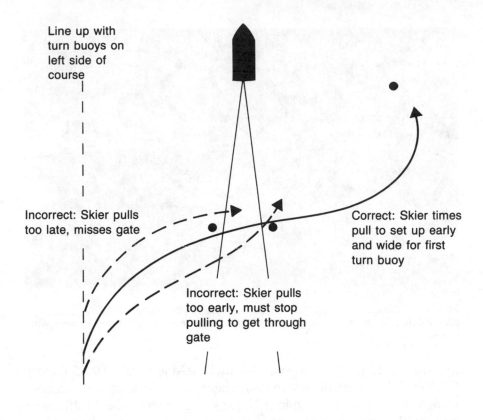

Line up with
turn buoys on
left side of
course

Incorrect: Skier pulls
too late, misses gate

Correct: Skier times
pull to set up early
and wide for first
turn buoy

Incorrect: Skier pulls
too early, must stop
pulling to get through
gate

Figure 9.7. Negotiating the entrance gate.

after pass through the slalom course. After each successful pass of six buoys, the boat speed is raised two miles per hour until the maximum speed for the division is reached. On each subsequent pass, the towrope is shortened in premeasured increments. This continues until the skier falls or misses a buoy or gate. The skier who rounds the most consecutive buoys is the winner (Figure 9.8).

The minimum starting speed for men and boys is 30 miles per hour. The minimums for senior, junior, and female divisions vary between 24 and 28 miles per hour. The maximum speeds are 36 miles per hour for men and boys and 34 miles per hour for most others. Once the skier has made a successful pass at the maximum speed, the 23-meter (75 feet, 5½ inches) towrope is shortened to 18.25 meters (59 feet, 10½ inches), then 16 meters (52 feet, 6 inches), 14.25 meters (46 feet, 9 inches), 13 meters (42 feet, 7¹³⁄₁₆ inches), 12 meters (39 feet, 4⁷⁄₁₆

Figure 9.8. Tournament slalom action. Photo courtesy of Tom King. Printed with permission.

inches), 11.25 meters (36 feet, 10⅞ inches), and finally 10.75 meters (35 feet, 3¼ inches). (Metric measurements are used to assure standardization with international rules.) Those skiers reaching the 11.25-meter and 10.75-meter shortenings are skiing on a rope that is shorter than the distance from the boat to the turn buoy! The difference must be made up entirely by reach.

There is one twist to this progression. Skiers may elect to start at a higher speed or shorter rope length. If their first passes at the higher speed or shorter rope length are perfect, the skiers continue and are credited with the points for the passes they skipped. If the skiers fall or miss a buoy on the initial pass, they receive credit for the buoys they rounded up to that point as if the pass had been performed at the minimum starting speed.

To assure accurate speeds, the towboat is timed through the course either by a stopwatch or an automatic timer. If the speed is faster than the allowable tolerance, skiers are granted the option of a reride (which the skiers normally take if they have missed or fallen during the pass). If the speed is slower than allowable, a reride for that pass is mandatory.

Five judges, one in the towboat and the others viewing from elevated stations near the course, rule on whether each buoy is rounded or missed. In the event of a disagreement, the majority rules. The boat judge and the two other judges with the best view of the gates rule as to whether the skier entered and exited through the gates.

Safety boats idle just outside the course to pick up fallen skiers and to render aid in the rare event of an injury. All skiers in the slalom event must wear ski vests.

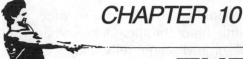

CHAPTER 10

THE FUN AND CHALLENGE OF TRICK SKIING

Trick skiing is the most artistic and creative of the three standard competition events. While both slalom and jumping involve skiing a more-or-less-fixed path through a course, trick skiing is free form. The tricks performed, their style, and how they are sequenced in a run are totally up to the skier. As in dancing, the emphasis is on grace, control, and economy of motion.

There are many different kinds of tricks, almost all of which consist of some sort of turn on one or two skis, from a quarter of a revolution (90°) to as many as two and one half revolutions (900°). Tricks done on the water are called surface tricks and those done in mid-air off the wake are called wake tricks.

Sideslides are surface tricks in which the ski or skis slide at a 90° angle to the boat for a short time. *Stepovers* involve stepping over the rope with a ski or free leg during the turn. The entire body passes over the rope during a *ski line* trick. *Toehold* turns are performed while the skier is towed by one foot in a toehold attachment on the rope. (Some top trick-skiers perform entire runs of toehold tricks without touching the handle with their hands.) *Somersaults* are either forward or backward flips off the wake. These basic kinds of tricks can be combined in various ways to result in some highly difficult and complex tricks, some of which require elaborate set ups or "wraps" to perform. Reverses, the same trick done by turning in the opposite direction, may also be performed.

Trick Skiing Principles

Trick skis are very easy to get up on. Because they are so wide, you pop up from a start with just a little bit of throttle. Once you are up, the finless skis will probably feel somewhat squirrelly, sliding around as if they had a mind of their own. This slippery feeling will go away after a while, as you discover how to control skis with the edges rather than with the fins.

Good skiing posture becomes even more important when you ride trick skis. Keep your back and head erect, your knees very bent, and your skis together. Ride your trick skis often and get used to them by cutting back and forth and jumping the wakes. When you are steady on your trick skis you're ready to try your first tricks.

The right boat speed is important for tricks. With too much speed, the skis will feel slippery and hard to control. With too little speed, the skis will be difficult to turn. Seek an intermediate speed that feels comfortable. Most adults will require a trick speed of between 13 and 18 miles per hour; skiers under 100 pounds may need to go as slow as 10 or 12 miles per hour. Once set, your driver should hold the speed as constant as possible.

All tricks, from the simplest to the most complex, require mastery of four key fundamentals. If you learn these fundamentals when you are learning the simple tricks, you will find that learning how to do the more advanced tricks later on will be much easier. If you ever have difficulty with a trick, chances are good that you are violating one or more of these basic principles.

- Keep your head up and your back erect. Any object that turns or spins does so around an axis, like the hub of a wheel or the poles of the earth. To turn smoothly on trick skis your upper body must remain upright, as if a rod were driven from your head down your back (Figure 10.1). Bend at the waist while turning and you become unbalanced, like a wheel that is out of round.
- Bend your knees. Except when springing off the wake during wake tricks, you should exaggerate the normal knee bend when trick skiing (Figure 10.1). This helps keep your weight positioned over your binders, lowers your center of gravity, provides shock absorption, and provides much greater stability because your entire leg, and not just your ankle, controls the ski.

Figure 10.1.   Keep your head up, back straight, and knees bent.

- Lead all turns with your head. Watch any athlete involved in a spinning action, like a gymnast, a springboard diver, or a figure skater, and you will notice that the rotation is initiated and guided with the head. When in motion, your body will tend to follow the lead of your head, which in turn follows where your eyes are focused. Keep your head erect and check yourself to be sure that you are leading each turn with your head and eyes (Figure 10.2). (While this principle holds in most cases and should be second nature to all trick skiers, some advanced skiers perform some 180° turns by twisting their leg or body and turning just the ski, while their head remains pointed forward.
- Keep the handle at belt level and in close to your body when turning. Unlike the gymnast, diver, or figure skater, the trick water-skier must contend with a towrope and handle. Pull the handle in by tucking your elbows in toward your hips when riding forward. When turning, the handle should be passed close to the back at the belt line. When returning to the front position, the arms should once again be tucked in and not allowed to be pulled out straight. This principle holds true for toehold tricks as well. The handle must be kept in close by the toehold leg.

Figure 10.2. Lead turns with your head, keep handle in close.

Trick Skiing Fundamentals
1. Head and back erect.
2. Knees bent.
3. Lead turns with the head.
4. Handle in close to body when turning.

Six Basic Tricks

There are so many tricks that to explain how to do them all would require another book. However, the following instructions for six basic two-ski tricks will give you a good introduction to the fun and challenge of trick skiing.

Two-Ski Sideslide

The first trick you should learn is the sideslide. In a sideslide the skis are turned 90° in either direction until they are sliding sideways to the boat. The sideways position is held for a moment and the trick is completed when the skis have returned to the front position. This trick is simple when you realize that trick skis are designed to slide sideways. Most beginners do not trust their skis and waste many falls until they learn through experience that their skis will slide and not catch.

The key to doing a successful sideslide is to turn the skis a full 90°. If you turn them only part way, you will begin to creep toward the wake and the skis will probably slide out from under you. If your skis are turned completely sideways, you will not experience a tendency to move toward either wake.

Get in a good ready position with your head up, back straight, knees well bent, and handle in (Figure 10.3a). Without letting go of the handle with either hand and without looking away from the boat, twist your hips and turn the skis until they are completely sideways and sliding (Figure 10.3b). (Turn to the side that feels most comfortable.) The ski on the side of the turn will rotate almost in place and the other will come out in front.

Lock into the slide position with your head up, back erect, and knees bent. Hold the handle in so close that it almost touches your hip. Spread your skis apart a little and stand on top of them without a significant lean away from the boat. Tilt the leading edges of the skis up slightly with your ankles (Figure 10.3c).

a

Figure 10.3. Sideslide (cont. on next page).

b

c

Figure 10.3. Sideslide (cont.).

To return to the front position, simply bring the handle around in front of you.

If you have trouble turning completely sideways and tracking straight, try letting go with the outside hand. Keep the handle in as close as possible by pulling the elbow of the rope arm in toward your hip, and extend the free arm for balance.

Two-Ski 180° Surface Turns: Front-to-Back and Back-to-Front

The key to the front-to-back turn is to be prepared to ski backwards. Skiers who first try this trick are often surprised at having gotten around backwards so easily, and they don't know what to do once they are there. The backward skiing position is essentially identical to the forward position (head and eyes up, back straight, knees bent); the only difference is that the handle is held close to the back at the belt line.

Use the overhand grip, that is, with the knuckles of both hands on top. From the front position the handle will naturally be twisted upside down by your rope hand during the turn, so that when it is regrasped by the free hand behind your back, the knuckles of both hands face down. On land, with your rope tied to a solid object, practice turning and grasping the handle. Imagine yourself skiing backwards.

On the water your objective is to reach this backward position smoothly. Assume the forward ready position (Figure 10.4a). Turn in the direction that is most comfortable by pulling the handle in firmly toward and past the opposite hip, leading the turn with the head, and rotating the hips and knees. Initiate the pull with both hands but release with the outside hand as the skis begin to turn. Keep the handle in very close and do not change the position of your body (Figure 10.4b). The turn is begun like a sideslide but must be continuous to the back position without any hesitation at 90°. Keep the skis together and parallel. In the back position quickly regrasp the handle at the small of your back (Figure 10.4c). This will be easy if you have held the handle in close during the turn. If it gets pulled away from the body, you will have to grope for the handle with your free hand, which will probably cause a fall. Be sure to keep your back erect and your head up, eyes on the horizon. Don't look down or bend forward at the waist.

If you fall, examine the fundamentals: Is your head up? Back straight? Knees bent? Skis together? Handle in close during the turn and regrasped by the free hand at the belt line?

a

b

Figure 10.4. Front-to-Back and Back-to-Front (cont. on next page).

c

d

Figure 10.4. Front-to-Back and Back-to-Front (cont.).

When you are successful at completing a front-to-back, ride there for a while to get used to skiing backwards. Keep your head up and the handle in close. To come forward, simply let go with one hand and keep the handle near your hip as the rope pulls you to the front (Figure 10.4d). Regrasp quickly in the front position and pull in before the handle gets pulled away from your body.

Two-Ski 360° Turn: Front-to-Front

The 360 is a continuous front-to-front turn. The most difficult part is passing the handle smoothly behind the back. It is most easily learned by doing two 180s in the same direction and then working to eliminate the hesitation until a complete turn can be made without stopping the skis in the back position.

Assume the ready position, then do a front-to-back and stop. Now, do a back-to-front, turning in the same direction. Do this over and over again concentrating on grasping the handle precisely.

Gradually shorten the amount of time that you spend in the back position before turning forward. When you can turn smoothly and pass the handle without fumbling, both 180s will blend into one 360° turn with the skis never stopping (Figure 10.5a-e).

When concentrating on handle passing, do not forget the other fundamentals. Be sure to keep the skis together throughout the turn. Do not let one get ahead of the other.

a

Figure 10.5.   Front-to-Front (360) (cont. on next page).

b

c

Figure 10.5. Front-to-Front (360) (cont. on next page).

d

e

Figure 10.5. Front-to-Front (360) (cont.).

Two-Ski 180° Wake Turns: Front-to-Back and Back-to-Front

The wake 180s introduce you to wake tricks. In all wake tricks the entire turn must be completed in mid-air off the boat wake. To do wake tricks you must find the sharpest, highest, and cleanest part of the wake at your tricking speed by adjusting the length of the rope. Trick ropes often have shortening loops spliced into them for this purpose. (Make sure that the weight in the boat is properly balanced, because this will affect the wakes.) Once you have found the right rope length, practice crossing the wakes while skiing backward to get the feel of them.

Begin the wake front-to-back in the center of the wakes. Edge briskly toward the wake. (Turn in the same direction as your first surface 180.) At the very crest of the wake and not before, spring up by straightening your legs and initiate the turn by pulling on the rope and leading with your head (Figure 10.6a, b). It's not necessary to leap high. If you time it right the wake will do the work. It is important, though, that you not turn before reaching the crest. The most common fault on wake tricks is turning too soon. The result is either that the skier falls or the skis never get into the air. Remember, the trick must be done in mid-air to count. In the air your body must be straight—head, back, and legs. Your handle should be held close and your skis kept together.

The momentum from your cut to the wake should carry you out beyond the outer curl of the wake so that you land on the flat water outside. (If you do not approach the wake fast enough, you will land on the curl and probably slide out.) Anticipate the landing. Grasp the handle with both hands and keep it close to your back (Figure 10.6c). Look up, not down. When you land, bend both knees to absorb the shock. If you land stiff-legged, you will bounce or slide out. Land leaning toward the wake slightly to bank the skis.

To do the wake back-to-front, gauge where the wake is by looking out of the corner of your eye (don't turn your head to look over at it) and cut toward it (Figure 10.6d). You will feel the wake as you begin to ski up it, but don't turn forward immediately. Wait a split second longer until you are at the very crest of the wake, then push off and lead the turn with your head (Figure 10.6e). If you turn too soon you will slide out on the wake. Keep the handle in close while in the air. On landing, bend your knees and tuck your elbows in toward your hips.

These six tricks are just the beginning. If you've gotten this far you're probably hooked on trick skiing and will want to learn more. From here you will go on to learn two-ski wake 360s and surface and wake stepovers. Then you'll relearn all of these tricks on one ski and move on to basic toehold turns. When you have these tricks mastered, you'll begin putting them together in simple trick runs.

As you advance, concentrate on the fundamentals and work to make your tricks clean and precise, like dancing on water. It will be helpful if you have someone take home movies or videos of your tricks. Knowing how you look, not just how you think you look, will make it much easier to improve your technique. If you practice hard, before long you'll be ready to try trick competition.

Trick Competition

In sanctioned competition, each trick skier makes two 20-second passes. The skier performs a different routine or run of tricks in each pass. Two buoys 15 meters (49 feet) apart mark the beginning of the trick course on either end. The skier may begin the run anywhere between the two entrance buoys. The run, beginning with the skier's first motion, is timed by a stopwatch and at the end of 20 seconds a horn or whistle is sounded. Each trick has a point value based on its difficulty. The points

a

Figure 10.6.   Wake Front-to-Back and Wake Back-to-Front (cont. on next page).

b

c

Figure 10.6. Wake Front-to-Back and Wake Back-to-Front (cont. on next page).

d

e

Figure 10.6. Wake Front-to-Back and Wake Back-to-Front (cont.).

for all tricks performed in both runs are added together to yield the skier's total score. Tricks may not be repeated for credit but reverses are permitted. The skier with the highest two-run point total is the winner.

The runs are scored by five judges who normally occupy separated elevated platforms on shore. The judges call out the tricks as they are performed and determine if they were done according to the rules. The judges use abbreviated names for the tricks and their recording secretaries use a special shorthand to write them down so that they can keep pace with the skiers who can sometimes perform a trick a second. The tricks are described by the position in which the skier lands ("front" or "back") and whether it is a wake ("wake"), stepover ("line"), toehold ("toe"), or some other variety of trick (Figure 10.7). Thus, a judge would call a simple trick like a wake 180 front-to-back a "wake back" (notation: WB), and a complex trick like a 540° wake toehold stepover back-to-front a "toe wake line five front" (notation: TWL5F). Prior to the event the skiers are required to submit to the judges a list of tricks that they intend to do.

Figure 10.7. An advanced one-ski wake trick. Photo courtesy of Tom King. Printed with permission.

Trick skiers select the boat speeds they desire, either by telling the driver at the starting dock or by signaling to the boat before entering the course. Once set, the speed must remain constant. The skiers may select different speeds for their second passes. They may start on two skis and drop one during either or both passes. A fall in the first pass does not preclude a skier from making the second pass.

One or two safety boats idle near the course during the event to pick up fallen skiers and dropped skis and to render immediate aid in case of an injury. Skiers who elect to use a towrope quick release device may select any person who is not an official in the event to ride in the towboat to operate the release. The use of personal flotation devices in the trick event is optional.

CHAPTER 11

CONQUERING THE JUMP RAMP

Learning how to jump is an accomplishment of which any skier can be proud. Although it may sound scary, skiing over "the monster," as the jump ramp is sometimes called, is not really as hard as it may seem.

Before attempting to jump you must be very stable and confident on two skis. You should be a good wake jumper, able to make long wake jumps in good control. The physical shock of a jump landing is not great but you should be able to jump from a 3-foot-high wall onto solid ground in good balance.

You must also have proper equipment. Use jump skis only, not regular skis or combo pairs, and a standard 75-foot single-handle rope. You should wear a properly sized ski vest, a helmet suitable for ski jumping (one that is designed for or has been used routinely by water ski jumpers, not a motorcycle or football helmet), and a pair of wetsuit shorts or a sturdy pair of cloth shorts over your swimsuit (Figure 11.1). Jump only when the water is calm.

A regulation water ski jump ramp (Figure 11.2) is 14 feet wide and 21 to 22 feet long above the waterline. The frame of wood or metal supports a deck of waxed plywood or fiberglass. Plywood safety aprons angle out from the sides.

Jump ramps are adjustable to different heights. When you are learning, the ramp should be set at 4 or 5 feet. The surface should be wetted down and cool before use. Tournament ramps have sprinkler systems to keep the surface wet during jumping events. Many ski clubs have jumping ramps for the use of their members and guests.

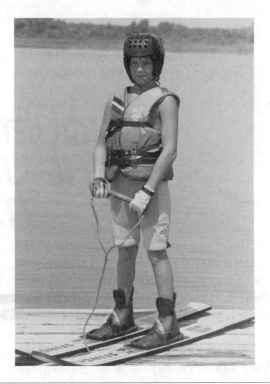

Figure 11.1. Well-prepared jumper wearing vest, helmet, gloves, and wetsuit shorts.

Figure 11.2. A regulation water ski jump ramp.

The Corner Jump

A method to introduce you to the feel of the ramp before going over the top is the corner jump. With this technique you ski over just the lower righthand corner of the ramp surface.

You should have a driver who is familiar with driving for jumpers and who can set an appropriate speed for you. Most adults will want a speed of 20 to 25 miles per hour. The boat should pass about 30 feet from the lower right corner at a 30° to 45° angle away from the ramp. The boat path and skier path are shown in Figure 11.3.

On your first corner jump you want to make contact with the ramp about 2 feet in and come off 2 feet up the side. Hit with your skis together and flat. If they are too far apart or on edge, they will slide out from underneath you when they hit the hard, slick surface.

Your body position in front of the ramp, on the ramp, and in the air is critical. Keep your head and back erect, knees bent, weight slightly forward and evenly distributed on the balls of your feet, skis close together, and handle in close to the waist with elbows tucked into your hips.

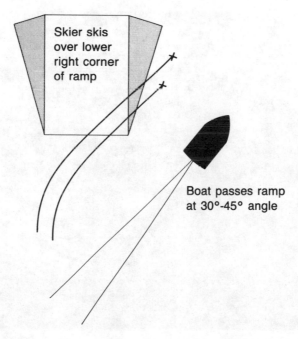

Figure 11.3.   The corner jump technique.

As you approach the ramp, ski out somewhat wider to the left than is necessary to reach your intended point of contact with the ramp. Stop pulling and as you begin drifting toward the boat, aim for the lower right corner. Freeze in position before and during the jump. Keep your ski tips up in the air. Absorb the landing with your legs but don't collapse (Figures 11.4a-d).

This first corner jump should feel little different from skiing over a large wake, and you should have no problem skiing away from it. Take a bigger bite on each successive jump until you are contacting the ramp 4 or 5 feet in and coming off 4 or 5 feet up the side. Concentrate on freezing in a solid jumping position throughout the jump.

Over the Top

A couple of corner jumps should help you get used to the feel of the ramp and remove some of your nervousness. If your corner jumps have been solid, it's time to go over the top.

a

Figure 11.4. Jumping the corner (cont. on next page).

b

c

Figure 11.4. Jumping the corner (cont. on next page).

d

Figure 11.4.   Jumping the corner (cont.).

The biggest reason many beginners do not ski away from their first jumps is not that it's difficult to do, but that they are not prepared for the one-two surprise that is waiting for them. The first surprise is the unfamiliar sound and feel of the skis hitting the ramp surface. With your corner jumping experience, hopefully the grating sound won't bother you. Remember also that at 20 miles per hour your skis are on the ramp for less than a second, so you should not worry about falling and hitting the ramp. Unless you fall or begin falling before you reach the ramp, it is unlikely that you will ever come in contact with the ramp surface.

The second surprise is the thrill of sliding off the top of the ramp into mid-air. Many first-timers are so wide-eyed when they come off the top that they forget to maintain their body position. Prepare yourself for the surprise of flying off the top edge. Because of your perspective when you approach it, the ramp will look ominously like a brick wall (Figure 11.5), but don't let this appearance fool you. The ramp is sloped away from you and your skis will slide up it very easily. In an instant you will be over the "wall" and flying unsupported through the air. This can be very startling the first time, and many jumpers fall due to the "Wow!" syndrome. One way to prepare yourself is to get on the ramp and walk up it from bottom to top to get a feel for what it will look like. On your first jump, you must concentrate on holding your body position on the ramp and in the air and not letting the thrill distract you. Later on, when you are making jumps consistently, you'll be able to more fully enjoy the sensation of flying.

Now the boat should pass parallel and close (20 to 30 feet) to the right side of the ramp. Once again you want to ski over the ramp while drifting toward the boat so that you are not leaning against the pull of the rope when you hit the ramp. To do this, pull out somewhat past the ramp to the left, get in proper jump position, and as you begin to drift back toward the boat, aim toward the lower left corner. You will ski up the ramp diagonally from the lower left corner to the upper right corner as shown in Figure 11.6.

Figure 11.5. The ramp looks like a wall when you approach it.

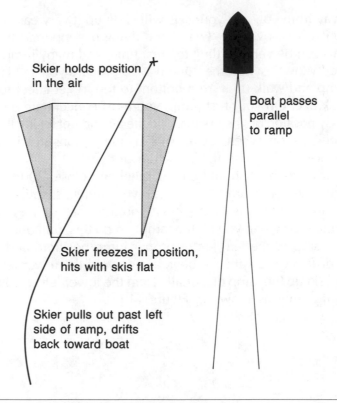

Skier holds position in the air

Boat passes parallel to ramp

Skier freezes in position, hits with skis flat

Skier pulls out past left side of ramp, drifts back toward boat

Figure 11.6. Boat and skier paths for first jump.

Freeze in position. Don't let your knees crush (buckle) as you go up the ramp but keep the same knee bend (Figures 11.7a, b). As you come off the top you will float momentarily then begin to drop. Force yourself to remain in position even though there will be slack in the rope. Keep the handle at waist level; don't raise it over your head. Because your skis are no longer supported by the ramp, you must consciously keep them together and the tips up. Avoid looking down or your ski tips will drop. Look ahead at the boat (Figures 11.7c, d).

Absorb the impact of landing as you would when jumping from a low wall. Land on the balls of your feet (Figure 11.7e). If you land with your weight on your heels, you'll collapse. Even if you hit your rump on the water when you land, don't give up; you may still be able to ride away if you hold on to the handle. To avoid having your arms pulled out, hold the handle with both hands and resist when the rope snaps tight.

a

b

Figure 11.7.   Over the top (cont. on next page)!

c

d

Figure 11.7. Over the top (cont. on next page)!

e

Figure 11.7. Over the top (cont.)!

If you don't ski away from your first jump, you probably will on one of the next few tries. If you are landing on top of the boat wake, move the boat out a few more feet. If you have a lot of trouble making a jump, go back to practicing corner jumps until you master holding your position in the air and making solid landings.

First Time Over the Jump Ramp

1. Keep head and back erect, handle in, knees bent throughout jump.
2. Contact ramp with skis close together and flat.
3. Keep skis together and tips up in air.
4. Absorb landing with knees.

Jumping Competition

In a tournament, each jumper is given three passes by the ramp. The skier may either jump or "balk" (ski by the ramp) on each pass. For a jump to count, the skier must ski away from the landing. The skier with the longest jump is the winner.

The boat must pass parallel to the right side of the ramp. Two lines of buoys, one 15 meters (49 feet, 2½ inches) and the other 19 meters (62 feet, 4 inches) from the side of the ramp, help the boat driver maintain a parallel path. The skier tells the driver how far from the side of the ramp he wishes the boat to go. Many skiers request "just outside" the 15-meter buoys or "split" between the 15-meter and 19-meter buoys. The skier can request any boat speed that does not exceed the maximum for his or her division. (Thirty-five miles per hour for most men's divisions, 30 to 32 miles per hour for most others.) The height of the ramp varies for different divisions—6 feet for Open Men, 5½ feet for Men I and Men II, and 5 feet for all others.

Because the boat speed cannot be greater than the maximum specified in the rules, most skiers employ the *double wake cut* to increase their own speed for more distance (Figure 11.8). As their boats approach the ramp, skiers first ski out to the left, then, timing their cuts in reference to buoys anchored a set distance from the ramp, cut far out to the right side of the boat, away from the ramp. The skiers wait until the very last moment before cutting back across both wakes and over the ramp. By cracking the whip in this fashion the best skiers can increase their own speed to nearly double that of the boat.

Speed is only one component of a long jump, however. If the skier's knees buckle under the stress of impact with the ramp, all advantage is lost. If, on the other hand, the skier springs up so that his or her legs are fully extended at the top of the ramp, the result is a spectacular long distance leap (Figure 11.9). Properly performed, a double wake cut and spring can land an Open Men division skier over 200 feet away from the ramp. With such great speed and with such great force on impact with the ramp, miscalculations can result in dramatic falls.

The jump distances are measured by a simple yet accurate system that uses the principles of triangulation. Three *jump meter* stations equipped with large protractors are set up on shore a known distance from the ramp and from each other. Operators at each station look through sighting devices on the protractors to the point where the skier lands. The sight lines create imaginary triangles between each meter

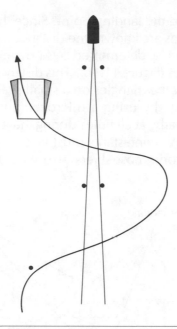

Figure 11.8.   The double wake cut.

Figure 11.9.   A double cut and spring can propel a jumper a great distance.
Photo courtesy of Tom King. Printed with permission.

station, the ramp, and the landing point. Since the distances between the three shore stations are known, the distance between the ramp and the skier's landing can be determined by knowing the angles between the legs of the triangles (Figure 11.10). This distance calculation is either made by reproducing the triangles on a small-scale "masterboard" or, now more commonly, by using a microcomputer.

Safety boats idle nearby at all times during the jumping event to assist if there is an injury. All contestants must wear ski vests and, although they are not mandatory, most skiers also wear helmets.

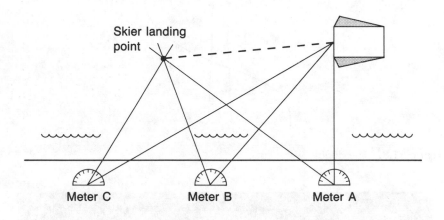

Figure 11.10. Determining jump distances by triangulation.

CHAPTER 12

SKI-LESS WATER SKIING

For many skiers, barefooting is the ultimate. Maybe this is because it seems impossible to ski on just the soles of your feet (Figure 12.1). But skiers as young as 6 or 7 and as old as 70 enjoy barefooting.

Barefooting does not require super strength, but you should be in good condition because with sudden falls at high speeds, your body can take a pounding. Even if you are in good shape, be well warmed up and limber before going barefooting.

Figure 12.1. Many skiers dream of being able to do this.

The equipment you need for barefooting is simple. Obviously you will need a fast boat. The speed you will need depends on your weight and, to some extent, the size of your feet. A simple formula to find your approximate barefoot speed is to divide your weight by 10 and then add 20 to the result. Thus, a 150-pound person would require about 35 miles per hour. Experiment with faster or slower speeds if you have difficulty learning.

For flotation and body protection it is best to wear a special barefoot wetsuit with extra thick neoprene on the back, chest, and rump and cinch straps on the legs to prevent water from entering. If a barefoot wetsuit isn't available, wear a close-fitting ski vest and a pair of wetsuit shorts or sturdy cloth shorts over your swimsuit. Use a standard length tournament quality towrope and handle. Barefoot only when the water is smooth.

The quickest way to learn how to barefoot is with the aid of a training boom, a bar that extends out from the side of the towboat. Unlike a towrope, a boom gives the skier something solid to hold on to for support and balance. However, since booms are expensive and require a good deal of driver experience to use safely, we will confine our discussion here to the most common methods.

Kneeboard Start

The easiest and least punishing method available to the average skier is the kneeboard start. This involves riding a kneeboard while seated and facing forward so that your feet can be dipped into the water at barefooting speed, allowing you to barefoot away from the board. Even if you are familiar with riding a kneeboard in the conventional manner, you may want to take a few rides in the seated position to get used to it.

Straddling the board in the water can be tricky. You want to position yourself so that your rump is just behind the center of the board and extend your legs forward. Lean back as the boat accelerates and guide the nose of the board with your legs. Sit up as soon as the board planes off (Figure 12.2a).

The key to riding a kneeboard in this position at high speed is to get far enough forward that the board does not bounce. While the boat is still moving slowly (10 to 15 miles per hour), move your rump forward so that your feet are resting on the nose of the board with your legs bent (Figure 12.2b).

When you are stable and comfortable, gently place your heels and arches in the water with your knees bent and your toes up. Signal to the boat to accelerate to your barefoot speed. Hold your breath as the boat accelerates because you will probably be completely covered by spray (Figure 12.2c). When you reach barefooting speed, rise up by pulling the handle in toward your waist and pushing on the water with your feet (Figure 12.2d). This action is much like being helped up from a sitting position on a floor. As you come up the board will be left behind, and your head will rise above the spray. Don't stand up too straight. Stay back with your feet in front of you, knees very bent, and your arms tucked in (Figure 12.2e).

Stepoff Start

The other method of learning how to barefoot involves stepping off a single ski at barefoot speed. The falls are harder with this method because you are in a standing position when you "go for it." Choose a ski with a flat bottom that will be steady at high speed. A concave or tunnel concave slalom ski can be used, but it is likely to be unsteady and difficult to step off of. Adjust the binder of the ski so that your foot will come out of it easily.

a

Figure 12.2. Kneeboard barefoot start (cont. on next page).

b

c

Figure 12.2. Kneeboard barefoot start (cont. on next page).

d

e

Figure 12.2.   Kneeboard barefoot start (cont.).

You will generally find the smoothest water for stepping off to be located in the curl just outside the wake. If the stepoff ski is on your right foot, ski just outside the right wake, and vice versa. At barefoot speed there will be little or no tendency to get pulled into the wake.

As you near barefoot speed, place the heel of your free foot in the water where the second ski would normally be (Figure 12.3a). As you put more and more weight on the foot, push it forward until it is 6 to 12 inches ahead of your other foot. Get down lower to the water. Keep your knees bent and your arms tucked in. Move the handle to one side so that it is directly in line with the foot in the water (Figure 12.3b). When you have transferred more than half of your weight to the foot on the water, it's time to go.

Quickly flick the ski to one side and thrust the second foot forward, even with the first foot, and hold on! Spray will cover you, but if you keep your feet out in front of you with your toes up and your knees bent, you'll soon come out of it (Figures 12.3c,d). The stepoff must be done quickly, but it must also be done smoothly. Any radical body movement will tend to sink the free foot and trip you.

a

Figure 12.3. Stepoff barefoot start (cont. on next page).

b

c

Figure 12.3. Stepoff barefoot start (cont. on next page).

d

Figure 12.3.   Stepoff barefoot start (cont.).

Using either of these methods, when you find yourself barefooting you may be so surprised that you lose your concentration. Pay attention to what you are doing or you'll experience that first rude "face plant" sooner than you expect. Stay down low at first. Later you will be able to straighten up and relax a bit (Figure 12.4). If you cross boat wakes or encounter rough water, get very low, lean back more, bend your knees more, and hold on tightly.

Barefoot Competition

In 1947 in Winter Haven, Florida, a teenager named A.G. Hancock became so proficient at skiing on miniature shoe skis that someone suggested that he didn't need any skis at all. Hancock tried it and became the first person in history to ski on bare feet. Barefooting quickly became part of the nearby Cypress Gardens ski shows and has since become a standard act in nearly every water ski show. For some reason the Australians fell in love with barefooting, and during the 1960s and

Figure 12.4. Proper barefooting position.

1970s they developed the first rules for barefoot competition. They hosted the first World Barefoot Water Ski Championship in 1978 and won the team title. In the same year, AWSA's American Barefoot Club was formed and the first National Barefoot Tournament was held in Waco, Texas. In 1986 the U.S. Barefoot Team defeated the Australians and won its first world team title.

Barefooting competition in the United States is divided into a number of age divisions for both sexes, and each summer there are local tournaments around the country as well as regional tournaments and a national championship. Every two years the United States Barefoot Team is selected to compete in the World Barefoot Water Ski Championship.

As originally developed by the Australians, there were four events in competition barefooting—wake slalom, tricks, start methods, and jumping. Later, start methods and tricks were combined. Today the three events of barefooting roughly parallel the three events of standard tournament water skiing.

The wake slalom event does not use a course of buoys. Rather, the skier gains points for the number of times he or she can cross both boat wakes in two 15-second passes. Crossings performed on one foot score higher than those on two feet; those done while barefooting backwards score higher than those done in the forward position (Figure 12.5).

The tricks event is quite similar to the tournament trick event. The barefooter is given two 15-second passes in which to perform as many tricks as possible. Tricks range from position tricks, like skiing on one foot or in a forward or backward toehold position (Figure 12.6), to tumbleturns, in which the skier goes down and spins around on his or her back and stands up again, to 180° and 360° surface and wake turns, and even to toehold turns.

Like tournament jumping, the object of barefoot jumping is distance, but the ramp is considerably smaller—18 inches high. Barefooters do not use a double wake cut but approach the mini-ramp straight on. *Barefoot jumping is strictly for the experts only. Don't try it unless you know what you're doing.*

Figure 12.5. Barefooting backwards.

Figure 12.6. Front toehold.

CHAPTER 13

WATER SKI TOURNAMENTS

Water skiing has a way of getting into your blood. Once you have a taste of what it's like to run the slalom course, do a trick run, make a jump, or barefoot, you may just decide to see how good you can become. When this happens, water skiing ceases to be merely a recreational activity. Instead it becomes a serious, competitive sport worth the effort required to achieve excellence (Figure 13.1). At this stage you'll want to start skiing in AWSA-sanctioned water ski tournaments.

Figure 13.1. Tournaments attract the hard-core water-ski enthusiasts. Photo courtesy of Tom King. Printed with permission.

The AWSA Competition System

Water ski competition in the United States is governed by the American Water Ski Association (AWSA). AWSA establishes the rules for sanctioned tournaments, performance rating levels for skiers in various age divisions, and standards for certifying tournament officials.

Each year hundreds of local tournaments are produced by water ski clubs around the country. The club hosting a tournament provides the water site, ski courses, and facilities, and arranges for the availability of tournament-certified towboats. The tournaments are officiated by rated volunteer judges, boat drivers, and scorers. Club members and skiers, along with their friends and family members, help out by serving as dock starters, registrars, pickup boat crews, trick secretaries, and announcers, and in other auxiliary positions.

Besides hoping to win a trophy, most tournament skiers also seek to exceed their own personal best performances, to achieve a higher skier's rating, and to qualify for the regional and national tournaments. Skiers may qualify for the National Championships by achieving certain Exceptional Performance (EP) standards in local tournaments during the year or by winning or placing in their regional tournament. (There are five AWSA regions.) Besides the tournament Nationals, there are two other national tournaments—one for barefooting and one for club show skiing.

While most tournaments award trophies or medals to the winners, some special tournaments offer cash prizes. These tournaments are generally restricted to the top-ranked Open Men and Open Women skiers and are sometimes produced for television (Figure 13.2).

Figure 13.2. Some top tournaments offer cash prizes. Photo courtesy of Tom King. Printed with permission.

Tournament water skiing is international, with a World Water Ski Championship held every other year under the auspices of the World Water Ski Union (WWSU), the international governing body of water skiing. Each member nation of WWSU may send a six-member team, comprised of both males and females, to compete in the World Championship. In the United States, team trials are held to select the United States Water Ski Team. Separate trials are held to select the United States Barefoot Team.

The dream of all tournament skiers is that water skiing will someday be a participating sport in the Olympic Games. Because of the recognition that this would bring to water skiing, leaders of the sport in this country and abroad are working diligently to make that dream come true.

How to Get Started

Skiing in tournaments is a lot of fun, and it's easier to get involved than you may think. If you can run the slalom course, do a routine of tricks, or jump, you might be eligible to enter a tournament near you. Don't be afraid of being outclassed by more experienced skiers at your first tournament. Many tournaments have special "novice" divisions specifically for those who have little or no experience skiing in tournaments.

The first order of business, if you are thinking about getting into competition, is to join the American Water Ski Association. Write AWSA (P.O. Box 191, Winter Haven, FL 33882) and ask for an application and information on current dues. When you join, request a copy of the tournament rules to look over.

Next, seek out and get to know the tournament skiers in your area. If there is a water ski club near you, sign up and begin attending their functions. AWSA will provide the addresses of clubs in specific local areas upon request to members. They can also help you start a club.

Upcoming sanctioned tournaments are listed in the official AWSA magazine and in annual tournament guides produced by each of the five AWSA regions. Attend a tournament or two as a spectator to get a feel for what goes on. Then when you are ready to ski in one, look for one that has scheduled novice divisions for the event or events you plan to enter. Enter before the deadline specified on the official entry form. You must pay an entry fee to the club (the amount will be listed in the tournament announcement) and sign a responsibility waiver that is part of the entry form. A parent or guardian must sign for a minor.

Arrive early at the tournament site to register and fill out any forms that may be required, such as an announcer's information sheet and a trick list if you are entered in tricks. Your AWSA membership card and skier's rating card (if required) will be checked at registration.

Review the schedule of events to see when your first event is; if a running order has been posted, look to see where you are in the lineup. Watch closely as the other skiers ski. Note where they start from for each event, what patterns the boats take, and where the skiers land when they are finished. Don't be afraid to ask questions. Most skiers and officials will be delighted to help a new tournament skier learn the ropes.

Before your event starts, be on hand at the starting dock to check in with the dock starter. Besides noting that you are present, the starter will safety-check your equipment and ask which of the available tournament towboat models you wish to use if you are tricking and what speed and rope length you wish to start at if you are slaloming. Be sure to be ready with your skis, ski vest, and whatever other equipment you use during the event well in advance of when you are scheduled to be up. Sometimes several skiers will not show up and are scratched from the running order, so you may be up a lot sooner than you expect.

When it comes your turn to ski, just relax. Everything may be new and unfamiliar, but the whole object is to have fun. So what if you fall? No one is going to laugh at you. You're not going to win any trophies the first time out anyhow, so just enjoy the experience. After a few tournaments the jitters will go away.

When you are finished skiing, be sure to get your rating card signed by the appropriate officials if you have achieved what you need for a rating. Then take time to congratulate yourself, because relatively few water-skiers advance to become tournament skiers.

FINAL THOUGHTS

It is hoped that this book has succeeded in helping you learn the basics of water skiing. Maybe by now you've caught water ski fever. That wouldn't be too surprising. Many people just like you have gotten hooked on the sport once they've had a taste of it and discovered that it's instant fun ("just add water").

For the water ski addict, there's this guarantee: You'll never get bored. There's always something new to learn, some new lake or river to ski on, new friends to make, and new equipment to try out (Figure 14.1). There are many ways to enjoy this wonderful world of water skiing. The choice is yours. Have a good, safe time on the water.

Figure 14.1. As a water-skier you'll always have new horizons to explore.

GLOSSARY

ALUMINUM HONEYCOMB—A honeycomb-like structure of aluminum cells used as a lightweight, stiff core in some fiberglass water skis.

APRON—The angled plywood side of a water ski jump ramp.

AQUAPLANE—A wide board towed directly by a powerboat, ridden in a standing or sitting position.

AWSA—American Water Ski Association, the governing organization for water ski competition in the United States.

BALK—In jumping, the skier's releasing the towrope and skiing past the jump ramp rather than taking a jump.

BARBELL PATTERN—A towboat pattern in which the boat runs back and forth on the same straight path.

BAREFOOTING—To water-ski on bare feet.

BAREFOOT WETSUIT—A special type of wetsuit for barefooting that has extra padding on the chest, back, and rump and cinch straps on the legs.

BEVEL—A rounded edge on a ski. Slalom skis are often beveled on the bottom edges, trick skis on the top edges.

BINDER—A rubber boot on a water ski to hold the skier's foot.

BLANK—A water ski sold without binders.

BOOM (TRAINING BOOM)—A bar extending to the side of the towboat from which a skier can be towed to learn new maneuvers.

BOW—The front of a boat.

BOWRIDER—A type of powerboat in which passengers can be seated forward of the driver.

BRIDLE—A part of the water ski towrope formed by the handle and the "Y" in front of it.

CABLE SKIING—Water skiing on a system that pulls the skiers by means of a moving overhead cable.

CARBON GRAPHITE—A reinforcing material used in some fiberglass water skis.

COMBINATION PAIR (COMBO PAIR)—A pair of recreational water skis, with one set up for use as a single slalom ski.

CONCAVE—The curved bottom on some types of slalom skis, which helps to hold the ski in tight turns.

CORNER JUMP—A technique for learning how to jump, in which the skier skis over only the lower corner of the jump ramp.

CRUSH—In jumping, the skier's knees buckling or bending when skiing over the jump ramp.

CURL—The curved side or base of a boat's wake.

CUT—To move from side to side behind the boat by tilting the skis on edge, leaning the body, and pulling on the towrope.

DIVISION—An age grouping for males or females in water ski competition.

DOCK STARTER—An auxiliary official at a water ski tournament who coordinates activities at the starting dock.

DOUBLE WAKE CUT—A technique used by tournament jumpers to increase their speed and hence their distance by "cracking the whip" across both wakes before skiing over the jump ramp.

DRYSUIT—A special suit for off-season wear designed to keep the skier warm and dry.

EARLY—In slalom, a skier's approaching a buoy with enough time to slow down and make a controlled turn.

EDGE—The side of a ski. To *edge a ski* means to tilt one edge of the ski into the water to accelerate or decelerate.

EDGE CHANGE—In slalom, a shift of the skier's weight that causes the ski to tilt from the outside to the inside edge. The transition between the acceleration phase and preturn (deceleration) phase of a slalom turn.

EP—Exceptional Performance Certificate, a performance standard in slalom, tricks, or jumping used as a qualification for the National Championships.

FIN—The rudder or skeg of a ski.

FREESTYLE—A type of water ski competition in which skiers perform somersaults and other tricks off the jump ramp.

GATE—A pair of buoys marking the beginning (and end) of the slalom course. The skier must ski through both end gates when running the course.

GUNWALE—The upper edge or deck on the side of a boat.

HAND PROTECTOR—A plastic or rubber stiffener where the rope enters the ski handle to prevent the rope from chafing or looping around the skier's fingers.

HIGH WRAP STRAPS—Rubber reinforcing straps which crisscross the ankles on a tournament-type ski binder.

HIT IT—The conventional voice command given by the skier to tell the towboat driver to accelerate the boat during a start.

HULL—The main body of a boat, the part of the boat in the water.

IDLE—Very slow speed.

INBOARD—A powerboat with a motor mounted inside the boat with a propeller shaft running through the bottom of the hull.

JUMP METER—A special angle-measuring device used as part of a system to determine jump distances at a water ski tournament.

JUMP RAMP—A large, floating inclined plane with a wood or fiberglass deck over which skiers ski in the jumping event.

JUMPER—A ski used for jumping. A skier who jumps.

JUMPING—A competition water ski event in which skiers leap for distance over a jump ramp.

KNEEBOARD—A water ski device resembling a short surfboard with a padded top that is ridden in a kneeling position.

LATE—In slalom, a skier's approaching a turn buoy without sufficient time to slow down and make a controlled turn. In jumping, a skier's waiting too long on a double wake cut and approaching the ramp with too much speed for a controlled jump.

MASTERBOARD—A device used as part of a jump metering system which recreates the jump meter angles on a small scale model.

NATIONALS—National Water Ski Championships.

NOVICE—A skier who has little or no tournament experience.

OBSERVER—A person in the towboat to watch the skier and assist the driver.

OPEN DIVISIONS—Open Men and Open Women, the competition divisions for the most skilled skiers.

OPPOSED GRIP—Holding the ski handle like a baseball bat with the palms facing in opposite directions.

OUTBOARD—A boat that is powered by an outboard motor. A motor mounted on a boat's transom which swivels to steer the boat.

OVERHAND GRIP—Holding the ski handle with the knuckles of both hands on top.

PFD—Personal Flotation Device. A ski vest or life preserver.

PITCH—The angle of the blades on a propeller.

PITOT TUBE—The water-pressure pickup tube of a boat speedometer system.

PLANE—To ride on top of the water.

PRETURN—In slalom, the phase of a slalom turn in which the skier slows down and prepares to turn at the buoy by changing ski edges and extending the handle.

PYLON (TOWING PYLON)—A post or tripod in the boat to which the towrope is attached.

PYRAMID—A water ski show act in which some skiers stand on the shoulders of others, two, three, or four tiers high.

QUICK RELEASE—A safety device that instantly disconnects the towrope from the boat when it is tripped by a person in the boat.

REGIONALS—Regional Water Ski Tournament.

REVERSE—In tricks, a trick that is identical to a basic trick except performed by turning in the opposite direction.

ROOSTER TAIL—A plume of water kicked up behind a boat or skier.

RUNABOUT—A small, powered pleasure boat.

SHORT-LINE—In slalom competition, running the slalom course on a shortened towrope after the skier's maximum division speed has been reached.

SIDESLIDE—A trick performed by sliding the ski or skis sideways.

SKIER'S SALUTE—A maneuver performed by lifting one ski off the water.

SLALOM—To ski on a single ski. The ski itself. A competition event in which skiers run a slalom course.

SLALOM COURSE—A standardized set of buoys that slalom skiers run in a zigzag fashion.

SPRING—To jump or leap up when skiing over the boat wake or jump ramp.

STEPOVER—A trick in which one ski (or the free leg) passes over the towrope during the execution of a turn.

STERN—The rear or back of a boat.

STERN DRIVE—A boat that is powered by a motor mounted inside the boat like an inboard but with a lower unit mounted on the stern that steers and tilts much like an outboard motor.

SWIM PLATFORM—A low platform extending from a boat's transom to assist swimmers and skiers getting into and out of the water.

SWIVEL SKI—A ski used in water ski shows with a special binder that allows the skier to turn around backward while the ski remains pointed forward.

TABLE—The area between the boat's wakes where the skier rides.

TAKE-OFF LOOP—A loop in a slalom or trick rope used for shortening the rope.

THROTTLE—The boat's accelerator control, usually a hand-operated lever.

TOEHOLD—A trick performed while the skier is towed by one foot in a toehold harness.

TOEHOLD HARNESS—A special handle-bridle attachment for trick skiing with a toehold strap into which the skier's foot can be inserted for toehold turns.

TRAINERS—A pair of small skis that are tied together and towed like a sled, used for teaching very young children how to water ski.

TRANSOM—The flat, upright part of a boat's stern on which an outboard motor is mounted.

TUMBLETURN—A barefoot trick in which the skier goes onto his or her back, spins around and stands up again.

TURNAROUND—A 180° or 360° turn on trick skis or on a kneeboard.

TYPE III—The U.S. Coast Guard's classification for certain approved wearable flotation devices, including most water ski vests.

WAKE—The V-shaped set of waves produced by a moving boat.

WETSUIT—A protective rubber suit that keeps the skier warm by allowing a thin film of water next to the body.

WHIP—To fling a skier outside the wake by turning the boat in the opposite direction.

WRAP—A type of maneuver used by trick skiers to prepare for certain multiple-turn wake or toehold tricks.

WWSU—World Water Ski Union, the world governing organization for water ski competition.

About the Author

Bruce Kistler, a nationally-known figure in the world of water skiing, began skiing at the early age of eight. By the time he was 13, he was skiing in local tournaments and soon moved on to regional and national championships.

In addition to performing the sport, Bruce served as executive director of the American Water Ski Association and organized the AWSA's American Barefoot Club. Also, many national organizations, including the American Red Cross and U.S. Coast Guard, have benefited from his expertise as an editorial consultant for their water ski publications. Author of numerous articles and booklets on water skiing, Bruce continues to be a freelance writer for such recreational publications as *Powerboat, Camping, Water Skiing Business*, and many more.

In his spare time, Bruce enjoys a variety of other outdoor activities, including canoeing and bicycling. He and his wife, Susan, live in Winter Haven, Florida, where Bruce works as a city planner.

By SAMMY DUVALL

SURVEYS of sports participation show that today there are nearly 11 million waterskiers in the United States. The American Water Ski Association reports that there are more than 400 water-ski clubs and that nearly 2 million new participants are attracted to this sport each year. You can be one of them.

Your preparations begin before leaving the dock, and always include the watchwords "safety first." Outfit your boat with life vests for everyone on board, plus the equipment required by state boating laws: paddles, a horn and a fire extinguisher.

Vests range from the inexpensive, orange horseshoe-shaped model that slips over the head and buckles around the back (about $12) to the four-buckle model that also gives unlimited protection to your rib cage, shoulders and kidney area (about $65). Make sure the vests fit correctly, and take special care when fitting infants and small children.

Many types of water skis are available today, but a combo pair made of fiberglass are the most durable and give the best performance. These skis are generally about 67 inches long and come with adjustable bindings fitting a wide range of foot sizes. Adjustable bindings are easier to put on and take off than other types. Prices range from $110 to $300 for a quality pair, depending on the brand.

Among the biggest problems beginning water-skiers face is getting control of the skis in the water. The skis have a tendency to float to the surface, which in turn forces the skier under water. Take some time in shallow water floating around and learning how to gain control of your skis.

When you're ready, the first step is the deep-water start. Don't try to pull yourself up. Be patient and let the boat do the work. As you begin to plane on the water's surface, slowly stand up. You need not hurry to stand straight up; let the boat's momentum pull you up. Your position checkpoints are: shoulders and back upright and perpendicular to the water's surface, elbows slightly bent, head up, knees bent and skis close together.

Your next challenge will be learning to control your skis while crossing

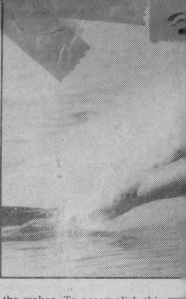

the wakes. To accomplish this, point your knees in the direction you want to go. For example, to go right, point your knees forward and to the right.

Now you're ready to move to one ski. Many water-skiers believe that the left foot should be forward while others prefer the right foot forward. You must determine for yourself what is best for you.

Slowly lift up one ski. Ski a short distance, then try the same procedure with the other ski. Whichever

Sammy Duvall is the reigning world overall water-skiing champion. If he wins the overall title at this weekend's 1988 United States Open, he will complete a sweep of the three major water-skiing championships.